SANTA▲FE▲DESIGN

Contributing Authors

Elmo Baca
Suzanne Deats

Publications International, Ltd.

Contributing Authors:

Elmo Baca is a lifelong resident of New Mexico. He holds a degree in architecture from Yale University and studied historic preservation at Columbia University. He participated in the revitalization of downtown Gallup and Las Vegas, New Mexico, and he is also a frequent contributor to *New Mexico Magazine.*

Suzanne Deats has been a resident of Santa Fe for 18 years. She is a nationally known columnist, whose articles on the arts regularly appear in *New Mexico Magazine.* She is a graduate of the University of New Mexico, and her artwork has been shown in galleries in Santa Fe, Los Angeles, and Tokyo.

PHOTO CREDITS

FRONT COVER: James Jereb Design/Lynn Lown Photography

Peter Aaron/Esto/Robert W. Peters, AIA: 57C, 67C, 73B, 86-87, 91B, 93B, 106, 107C, 139B, 140C, 157T, 158-159, 165C, 168T, 171C
Alison Abraham/Berry Langford Architect: 114T
Ed Berry/The Shop: 130, 248LR, 250LL, 250LR
Blue Raven: 230LL
Edmund A. Boniface: 220LL
Len Bouche: 4LC, 26LR, 27RC, 31B, 34LR, 35C, 36T, 43B, 43C, 100-101, 139T, 185LC, 188B, 191B, 204T
L.D. Burke III: 222TR
Channing-Dale-Throckmorton: 16B, 199TL
Blair Clark/Museum of International Folk Art: 29LR, 216, 232T, 233TL, 234TL, 234TR, 235LL, 251T
Blair Clark/Museum of New Mexico: 185LR, 190LL, 191TL, 191TR
Conlon/Moreno Gallery: 228LL
Counter Point Tile: 118T, 143, 144, 145C, 145LR, 147
Cristof's: 201TR, 211
David Cunningham: 217
Dell Woodworks Inc.: 224TR
Lisl Dennis/McHugh, Lloyd & Associates, Architects: 97TL, 97TR
Dewey Galleries: 175TL, 232C, 243C
Linda Durham Gallery: 192T, 228LR
Pamela D. Earnest Interiors: 60T, 60B
Richard L. Faller/Earnesto Mayans Gallery: 242TL, 247TR
Fenn Galleries, Santa Fe: 226LR, 237, 240B, 241TL
Laura Gilpin/University of New Mexico General Library: 40C, 40B
Kirk Gittings/Syntax: 34T, 39, 42T, 42B, 45, 46T, 47T, 47B, 48-49, 49C, 52, 53LL, 54, 55, 56-57, 58, 59, 60-61, 69LL, 69LR, 75, 77, 78, 82-83, 87T, 88, 89T, 91T, 93C, 94B, 96-97, 98, 103, 105T, 105B, 109, 110, 111T, 111C, 112-113, 115, 118LL, 119, 126T, 128-129, 131, 133B, 135, 138, 148, 149, 151T, 151LL, 153LR, 160-161, 162, 167LL, 167LR, 189LL, 190LR, 194, 226LL, 232B, 235TL, 235TR, back cover (TR, C, LL, LC, LR)
Kirk Gittings/Syntax/Collection Pecos Monument: 223C
Peter Gould and Hillary Riggs: 218T
Peter Gould: 224B
Don Gregg/Jan Beauboeuf: 229T
Hand Graphics Gallery: 243T, 244B, 245TL
Hawthorne Studio: 225T, 225C
Larry Horton: 44, 80B, 92, 113T, 133T, 134T, 161T, 164, 166, 167T, 168C
Larry Horton/Robert W. Peters, AIA: 80B, 171T
Larry Horton/Studio Arquitectura: 94T, 94-95, 104-105, 116-117, 124-125, 125TL, 171B
Elaine Horwitch Galleries: 245C
Harvey S. Hoshour/Hoshour & Pearson, Architects: 38B
Frank Howell Gallery: 246B
Jerry Jacka: 10TL, 10TR, 10C, 15LL, 15LR, 22TL, 22TR, 22LL, 29LL, 174T, 174B, 175TR, 175TC, 175LR, 176LR, 177TL, 180, 183T, 183LC, 183LR, 184TR, 184C, 184B, 185T, 186T, 186LC, 186B, 187TL, 187TR, 188T, 189T, 192C, 193TL, 195, 197T, 198TL, 198TR, 198C, 198B, 199TR, 199C, 200LR, 201B, 204C, 204B, 205TL, 205TR, 205B, 206TL, 206TR, 207TL, 207B, 208B, 209TL, 214, 215TL, 215TR, 215B, 226C, 227TL, 227TR, 227B, back cover (LC, RC)
Jerry Jacka/Heard Museum: 10B, 22LR, 172, 174C, 175LL, 176T, 176LL, 177TR, 177TL, 177LR, 178LL, 178LR, 179TL, 179LL, 179LR, 182TL, 182TR, 182LL, 182LL, 210, 212T, 212C, 212LR, 213TL, 213TR
Jerry Jacka/Museum of New Mexico: 189LR
The Jamison Galleries: 239TL, 239B, 240T, 240C, 241TR, 241B
Janus Gallery: 228TL, 231TR
James Jereb Design/Lynn Lown Photography: 49T, 65, 66, 70, 71, 72, 99, 123, 129B
Johnson Nestor Mortier & Rodriguez, Architects: 37B, 47C, 50T, 67LR, 83T, 84T, 84C, 85, 118LR, 122, 126LL, 134LL, 140B, 151LR, 153TL, 153TR, 154C, 156-157, 173, 200T, 221TR, back cover (TL)
Kailer-Grant Designs: 87B, 101T, 120-121, 140T
Gordon King/Santa Fe East: 206LL, 209B, 244T
C. Eugene Law/Charles-David Interiors: 69T, 125TR
LewAllen/Butler Fine Art: 231B
Herb Lotz/Ventana Fine Art: 245LR
Pegg Macy/Novak & Associates: 19LR, 28B, 34LL, 35T, 35B, 37C, 64, 153LL, 159B
Mariposa/Santa Fe: 207TR, 208C
Dave Marlow: 79T, 79C, 89LL
Linda McAdoo Galleries, Ltd.: 243B
McHugh, Kidder Architects: 49B
McHugh, Lloyd & Associates, Architects: 53C, 76C

Michele Monteaux/Museum of International Folk Art: 28TL, 29TL, 202T, 203TR, 222C, 222B, 234LR
David Muench: 4T, 5T, 5LR, 6C, 7LL, 7LR, 11, 12, 13, 14, 15T, 16T, 17, 18, 21, 23, 24B, 25, 26T, 32RC, 32B
Munson Gallery: 242B, 245TR
Museum of Fine Arts/Museum of New Mexico: 238T, 238B, 239TL
Museum of International Folk Art: 222TL
Museum of New Mexico: 29TR, 32T, 178TL, 178TR, 179LL, 191C, 200LL, 202TL, 203TL, 213LL, 213LR
Dan Namingha: 247B
The Native Market: 248LL, 249TR, 251B
Mark Nohl/New Mexico Economic & Tourism Dept.: 4LL, 4LR, 5LL, 6T, 6LL, 6LR, 7T, 9, 19T, 20TR, 24T, 26LL, 27T, 27LC, 30B, 32LC, 33, 36B, 37C, 38T, 40T, 41C, 43T, 89LR, 145LL, 146T, 146LL, 154T, 184TL, 188C, 190T, 196-197, 199B, 201TL, 202LL, 203LL, 203LR, 212LL, 226T, 230LR, 233LC, 233LL
Mark Nohl/Sombraje Collection: 141, 218B, 218C, 219TL, 219B, 220C, 221TL, 223T
John Olsen/Kells and Craig Architects, Inc.: 53T, 68T, 83B, 132-133, 134LR, 150, back cover (TC)
Jack Parsons: 50LL, 50LR, 73TL, 73TR, 74, 84B, 90-91, 93T, 97B, 101B, 102B, 107B, 114B, 114C, 116B, 125LR, 136-137, 154-155, 181, 233TLL, 251C
Robert W. Peters, AIA: 81B, 126LR, 146LR, 161B, 169
Robert Reck/Hayslip Design Associates: 163
Robert Reck/Mariposa/Santa Fe: 192B, 208TL, 209TR
Robert Reck/McHugh, Lloyd and Associates, Architects: 50-51
Robert Reck/Robert W. Peters, AIA: 80T, 102T, 113B, 139C, 154B
Robert Reck/Taos Furniture: 220T, 221B
Robert Reck/Thomas Hudson-Reidy Architect: 57T, 57B, 79B, 121T
Robert Reck/Van H. Gilbert Architect: 81T
Rettig y Martinez Gallery: 228TR
Anthony Richardson/Mariposa/Santa Fe: 208TR
Dolona Roberts Gallery: 236
Pedro Romero: 229LL
Jerry Rose/Novak & Associates: 8
Running Ridge Gallery: 193TR, 229LR, 249B
School of American Research: 20TL, 183RC
Shidoni Foundry and Gallery: 230T, 231TL
Beverley B. Spears, AIA: 31TL, 152, 165C, 248T
Studio Arquitectura: 116T, 170-171
Eric Swanson/The Native Market: 248C, 249TL, 250T
Jerry Teale/University of New Mexico General Library: 41B
William Teetzel: 219TR, 220LR
Tom Tennies/Novak & Associates: 185RC, 186RC, 187C, 187B
Kent/Tennies/Hoshour & Pearson, Architects: 38C
Michael Tincher/Presden Gallery: 246C
21st Century Fox: 238LC, 238RC, 244C
Ventana Fine Art: 193B, 247TL
Tony Vinella & Jody Blagden/Carter/Satzinger, Architects: 28TR, 67T, 67L, 76T, 76B, 111B, 142, 168B, 223LL
Wagner Gallery: 224TL, 225B
Nancy Hunter Warren: 30T, 30C, 31TR, 62, 108, 233RC, 234LL, 235LR
Peter Weiss: 27B
Peter Weiss/Bruce Davis Architect & Karen Terry, Designer: 41T, 68LL, 68LR, 129T, 159T, 165T
Wiggins Fine Art: 239C
Ben Wittick/Museum of New Mexico: 19LL, 20B
Tom Yee/Robert W. Peters, AIA: 63, 107T, 121B, 127, 145T, 157B

KEY

Numbers indicate pages.

T — Top	R — Right	LC — Left Center
C — Center	TL — Top Left	LL — Lower Left
B — Bottom	TR — Top Right	LR — Lower Right
L — Left	RC — Right Center	

TABLE OF CONTENTS

SANTA FE LIFE   4

ORIGINS OF SANTA FE DESIGN   8

SANTA FE ARCHITECTURE   44

CASA SANTA FE   62

Entradas 64	Cocinas 108	Baños 142
Salas 74	Lugares de Retiro 122	Portales 148
Comedores 98	Alcobas 130	Jardínes 162

SANTA FE ARTS   172

Baskets 174	Kachina Dolls 210	Santos 232
Pottery 180	Furniture 216	Paintings and Prints 236
Textiles 194	Sculpture 226	Folk Art 248
Jewelry 204		

SANTA FE DESIGN RESOURCES   252

INDEX   255

SANTA FE LIFE

Spruce Tree House, Mesa Verde National Park

Land Office Building, Santa Fe

Truchas Peak and Cemetery

Wheeler Peak, highest point in New Mexico

The name Santa Fe conjures up a flood of beautiful images. Many people who visit this charmed spot fall in love with the place and begin to dream about what it would be like to live here. Santa Fe touches the mind and the spirit through the senses. There is a natural connection that has to do with the clarity of light as it illuminates the landscape. Most people no matter who they are or where they come from are influenced at a basic level by the quality of light in Santa Fe.

In winter snow falls, but then the sky clears and the sun sparkles. Endless gray winter days are unknown here, and the winter sun can shine brightly day after day. Light, powdery snow discovers narrow ledges on the face of a butte, outlines the branches of the aspens, and etches patterns on canyon walls that had seemed perfectly smooth in summer. Deep snow masks the roughness of the land, burying sagebrush under soft mounds and enfolding the pine trees in robes of white.

Winter is the season for long, quiet hours of work. Thousands of Santa Fe artists and craftspeople spend the winter working at their easels, benches, looms, and potter's wheels, producing the art and fine crafts that make this area an important art center. This productive time is precious; it allows artists to renew their spirits as well as their stocks of work before the tourists and art patrons return.

Spring comes suddenly to Santa Fe. It almost seems as though all in one morning the snow melts, and the desert blooms in a delicate array of subtle color punctuated here and there by bright red cactus blossoms. Spring is a celebration. The arroyos swell with tumbling water from melting snow. Roads become a rich, muddy adventure. In town the air is filled with the scent of lilacs. In the mountains the distinctive fragrance of sap rising in the piñons perfumes the air.

In summer there is a dry edge to the days that is often relieved by a brief afternoon shower, which leaves behind a miraculous double rainbow or a rich red sunset that is incredibly complex in its many layers of color. All summer long, Santa Fe is busy with visitors from every corner of the world who come to explore the arts, as well as the culture that gave rise to them, and to enjoy the nearby wilderness.

Rio Grande

Sangre de Cristo Range

Horseshoe Lake, Sangre de Cristo Range

Santa Fe Plaza

Hondo Canyon, Sangre de Cristo Range

Indian Market draws the best artists and craftspeople to the Plaza for two days in August. There is brisk competition for the prizes and a crush of serious collectors vying for work by their favorite artists. Spanish Market is a similar event also held in August. The Santa Fe Opera and the Chamber Music Festival fill the summer air with music, and the local museums, most of which have been incorporated under the umbrella of the Museum of New Mexico, offer visitors the full spectrum of Santa Fe art, past and present.

The summer season used to end on Labor Day weekend, but now tourists visit Santa Fe throughout the year because they have discovered the pleasures of other seasons. Autumn crackles with brilliant color. The aspen leaves and chamisa blooms are a varied study in the color yellow. A walk in the country reveals a natural world like no other: glittering stones of every hue, plants of every imaginable form.

Costume competition, Santa Fe Indian Market

Palace of the Governors, Santa Fe

In early September the community turns out for its hometown celebration, Fiesta de Santa Fe. There are parades and religious observances honoring the peaceful reconquest of Santa Fe by Spanish colonists in the late seventeenth century. In October several small communities of artists host studio tours, and Rancho de las Golondrinas, a fully restored Spanish hacienda in nearby La Cienega, offers a fall harvest festival.

La Cienega

Rio de las Trampas, Pecos National Monument

White House Ruin, Canyon de Chelly National Monument

ORIGINS OF SANTA FE DESIGN

Santa Fe is the heart and soul of the Southwest—a vast and beautiful land that is something of a paradox. People have lived in the Southwest longer than they have lived anywhere else in the United States, but even today parts of the region are still almost unsettled frontier. The bold, dramatic landscape seems undisturbed by the people who have lived here during the last two thousand years. In Santa Fe the rough diversity of the Old West combines with the modern American concerns for history and the environment. Nature and civilization blend together in a complicated harmony that is influenced by its Indian, Spanish, and frontier heritage and blessed by the astounding natural beauty of the Rio Grande valley.

Three hundred miles west of Santa Fe, the raging Colorado River cuts a wide swath of terraced gorges, buttes, and canyons, known as the Grand Canyon. Near Santa Fe, the placid Rio Grande was tamed by the Indians to nourish fields of corn and beans. To the north, towering red sandstone formations and the snow-capped southern Rocky Mountains form a natural barrier that isolates and protects the region. To the south, the vast Sonoran desert is hostile to all forms of life except the most intrepid plants, animals, and humans.

This land is not only beautiful, but it has also provided for the needs of the people who have made the region their home. The Sangre de Cristo Mountains, which surround Santa Fe, are a haven for elk, deer, beaver, eagles, coyotes, foxes, and mountain lions—animals that have been hunted and also worshiped through the ages. Adobe clay mortar was plentiful for building. Cottonwood, ponderosa pine, fir, spruce, willow, aspen, and cedar stand ready to be cut and shaped into useful objects or used as fuel. Native American plants— corn, beans, squash, and chiles— provide not only sustaining food but also a complex and pleasing cuisine. There is yucca for sandals and baskets; cotton for clothing; silver and turquoise for jewelry and sacred objects.

While the arrival of each new group of people has brought new religions, new ways of living, and new building techniques to the region, the basic elements of life in and around Santa Fe have remained pretty much the same for hundreds of years. New ways have been incorporated, but the beauty of nature and its bounty have kept the long history of the region from being eclipsed. Santa Fe is a rich blend of cultures and natural influences that welcomes diversity without denying its own heritage.

Stone tools, including an axe, a pottery anvil, and an arrow shaft straightener

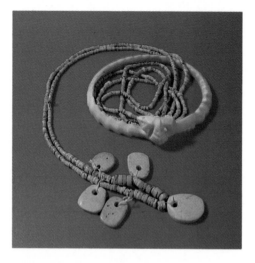

Hohokam carved shell bracelet and turquoise necklace

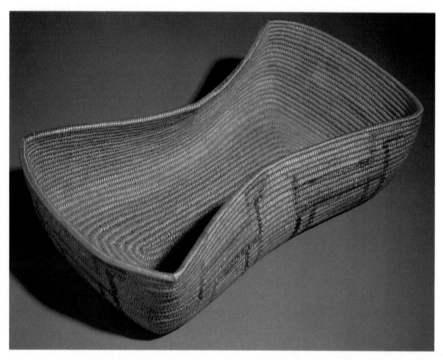

Anasazi basket that once belonged to a medicine man or shaman

Anasazi and Hohokam figures, bowl, and turquoise pendant

ANASAZI HERITAGE

Santa Fe design begins with the Anasazi, the ancestors of the modern Pueblo Indians and some of the first people to live in what is now New Mexico. *Anasazi* is a Navajo word that means "old ones." These people lived on the Colorado Plateau about two thousand years ago. They were the descendants of nomadic Basket Maker tribes that had lived in the desert. By 300 A.D. these people had learned to grow corn, squash, and beans. They built shelters by digging pits in the ground and covering them with roofs made of logs, sticks, leaves, and mud. A fire pit provided warmth and light inside these lodges.

About this time the Anasazi also began to make pottery, and by 700 A.D. they had developed a distinctive style of fired gray pots with painted black designs, which resembled the geometric lines, circles, dots, and animal forms that had ornamented their baskets. This style differentiates Anasazi pottery from pots made by people in other regions. Hohokam people living in the southern desert of Arizona made buff-colored pottery and decorated it with red designs. The people in the mountains made brown vessels trimmed with red and imprinted with rhythmic patterns made by bone tools. The Mimbres tribe in southwestern New Mexico painted stylized birds, animals, and humans on their vessels.

More than one thousand years ago, the Anasazi began to live in villages. They wore clothes made from animal hides and plant fibers. Their hunting and farming tools were made of stones, sticks, and sinew. They grew cotton along with their food crops and hunted with bows and arrows as well as spears and atlatls (a device for throwing spears). The people also built extra-large pit houses, or kivas, in which they gathered to dance, chant, and worship.

Pit house, Mesa Verde National Park, Colorado

Mesa Verde

Over time, the Anasazi began to build houses by stacking flat stones to make walls that were then held together with mud. They no longer dug their homes into the earth but built square and rectangular rooms above ground. They made roofs by placing logs across the tops of walls. These beams were then covered with sticks, brush, and mud. Rather than building separate houses and storerooms, the people linked their houses together into pueblos, which are very much like modern apartment houses. In Spanish, the word *pueblo* means both "village" and "people."

Santa Fe architecture is continually inspired by the Anasazi cliff dwellings at Mesa Verde, a plateau in southwestern Colorado. These magnificent structures were built between 1000 and 1275. When you look at these splendid towns, you see that the Anasazi accomplished a perfect blending of natural beauty with human needs and a human aesthetic. The structures conform to the rock in which they are built. Forming an organic link to the rock, they seem almost to become one with the earth. But the cliff dwellings are also very much human homes. They are intensely geometric and set themselves apart from nature by the power of their grand design and structure.

The Anasazi fully exploited the technical and artistic possibilities of masonry architecture to build the cliff houses of Mesa Verde. Cliff Palace, one of the major structures, sits beneath an immense natural stone canopy. It is a marvelous combination of rectangular and curved forms that are broken at unpredictable and unexpected intervals by window openings and roof-beam sockets. With its daring conical and square towers, Cliff Palace is a more exciting architectural statement than many of the homes you see in Santa Fe today. These rectangular modern buildings seem to be little more than poor imitations of Anasazi masterpieces.

Even if some Santa Fe buildings may not be worthy of their Anasazi heritage, you see the direct influence of the cliff dwellings on all Santa Fe architecture. Most buildings here are built in harmony with nature, using earth-colored masonry and massive, stark walls. Structures fit the earth; they are designed to complement and not obstruct nature. Adobe architecture blends in with the juniper, piñon, and sage that surround it, adding shades of salmon and ocher to the sub-

tle colors of nature to create a striking tapestry. Like many Santa Fe homes, Anasazi buildings also used solar orientation and thermal mass to make them comfortable all year round under rapidly fluctuating weather conditions.

The villages that the Anasazi built in the canyons of Mesa Verde stood silent for more than five hundred years. In 1874 William Henry Jackson, a pioneer photographer, rediscovered the cliff dwellings. His first photographs of Mesa Verde were published two years later, but the area was so remote that it was many years before the pueblos could be carefully studied and properly protected. Benjamin K. Wetherill, a local ranger, located the major ruins within the mesa during the 1880s. But Congress did not pass the federal antiquities act establishing Mesa Verde National Park until 1906. Protection by the Department of the Interior and the park service ended the indiscriminate digging, looting, and vandalism that might soon have destroyed these architectural treasures. The national park has also served to make Cliff Palace, Spruce Tree House, Mug House, Long House, and the other villages of Mesa Verde familiar to millions of Americans.

Doorway in Cliff Palace that was built to allow easy access for a person wearing a pack

Spruce Tree House, Mesa Verde National Park, Colorado

Cliff Palace, Mesa Verde National Park

Masonry wall, Chaco Canyon National Monument, New Mexico

Kivas, Chaco Canyon National Monument

Chaco Canyon

One hundred miles south of Mesa Verde in Chaco Canyon, Anasazi also built an interconnected network of twelve major pueblos and hundreds of smaller sites. Settlement began in the canyon, which is in northwestern New Mexico, in about 950 A.D. Eventually more than 7,000 people lived in this eight-mile-long canyon, making it the major urban center of the Southwest at that time.

Pueblo Bonito is the largest structure in Chaco Canyon. In fact, until the 1880s this 800-room pueblo was the largest apartment house in the world. (In 1882 a larger one was built in New York City.) Pueblo Bonito is laid out in the shape of the letter *D*. It is five stories high and housed more than 1000 people. The height of the pueblo's cubical and conical geometry is balanced by several deep kivas in its forecourt plaza.

Religious ceremony played a paramount role in the lives of the people who lived in Chaco Canyon. The kivas that they built are often 60 feet across. The people gathered in these huge subterranean cylinders to pray and dance. Although they left behind no written record of their world, the Anasazi make themselves and their religion known to us through their architecture, the decoration on their pottery, and their rock drawings (petroglyphs). Their reverence for all life is clearly evident in their stylized drawings of people, birds, snakes, deer, and their masked deities, the kachinas. The power of these symbols is evident. Even today when Anasazi images appear on everything from T-shirts and menus to furniture and wrought-iron sculpture, their primitive transcendence continues to startle us by revealing the soul of each living creature.

In addition to the legacy of the great kivas, Chaco builders left behind magnificent stone walls. These immense rock walls are made of alternating courses of large, rectangular stones and small chink stones. The walls at Chaco are the ultimate architectural expression of the integrated and precise geometric design that you see on a smaller scale in Anasazi pottery. Even today when many of these walls are in ruins, the thoughtfulness with which they were constructed is evident, and Santa Fe architects continue to use this kind of stone-wall mosaic to enhance their buildings.

Pueblo Bonito, Chaco Canyon National Monument

Petroglyphs, central Arizona

Anasazi petroglyphs, northern Arizona

15

Adobe wall

PUEBLO HERITAGE

During the thirteenth century the Anasazi left their splendid rock palaces and established new villages in other parts of the Southwest. No one knows for sure why the people abandoned their homes. We know that there was a twenty-three-year-long drought during the last quarter of the century. This hardship may have initiated the migration, or perhaps continued harassment from the Shoshonean tribes had made life in the cliffs too hazardous. Once they had left the high plateaus, the Anasazi wandered until they came to the highlands of the Rio Grande. Settling near the river, the people adapted their culture to this new environment. They changed from rock builders to earth builders, making their new homes from sun-dried clay rather than ledge stones. They became the Pueblo tribe, but they kept their sacred images and many of their crafts and customs. And they built new clan kivas and plazas in which to dance.

Not all the Anasazi settled near the Rio Grande. The Hopi villages of northeastern Arizona and the Zuni villages of northwestern New Mexico were also established in the thirteenth century. The three tribes—Pueblo, Hopi, and Zuni—are related by blood, language, dress, architecture, and religious practices, but each developed distinct decorative styles, customs, and dances. When you look at a pot from Acoma Pueblo, you see immediately that it is different from a pot from a Hopi or Zuni village, but you also see that it is a variation on a common theme. The pot is the product of centuries of gradual design evolution that has resulted in its particular motif and colors.

The new environment of the Rio Grande highlands required a new architecture. The people continued to build modular apartment houses, but the builders now used clay, dried and tempered by the sun, to build their pueblos. The Spanish called this sun-dried mud *adobe,* using an Arabic word. Walls that were as tall as seven stories were handbuilt layer by layer; adobe bricks were introduced to the Pueblos by Spanish colonists who had learned to make them from the Moors.

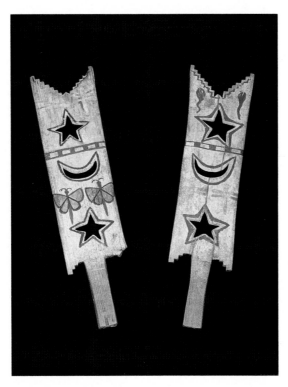

Zuni dance wands

Kiva and south pueblo, Pecos National Monument, New Mexico

This new building material gave the builders greater plastic and sculptural flexibility than the stones they had used before. They seem to have built their adobe pueblos not only to function as housing but also to evoke the surrounding landscape. The Rio Grande pueblos are man-made mountains that mimic their natural surroundings—the Sandia, Jemez, and Sangre de Cristo mountains.

Because the Anasazi were smaller than modern people, pueblo doorways seem low. Most rooms have only one entrance through an opening onto the central plaza of the pueblo or a smoke hole in the ceiling through which a ladder protrudes. Windows are few and tiny. The floors are packed earth, and ceilings were made by embedding poles into the top of walls to span the width of a room. These poles, or *vigas,* are tree trunks that are six to ten inches in diameter from which the bark has been removed. *Latillas,* or small branches, are placed across the *vigas,* covered with grass and brush, and plastered down with mud. Several inches of packed earth cover the layer of mud. By carefully positioning the vertical bearing walls, builders could add rooms to their apartment houses either horizontally or vertically.

Vigas and small square window openings, Taos Pueblo

House interior (1890s), Zuni Pueblo

Bread oven, Isleta, New Mexico

Bread oven and pueblo, Taos Pueblo, New Mexico

Prehistoric Pueblo pot

Kiva, San Juan Pueblo, New Mexico

Ka-k'ok-shi, or Good Dance (June 19, 1897), Zuni Pueblo

As their population increased, the people built additional pueblos. These separate apartment houses were unattached but linked spatially and spiritually to each other and the landscape. The space between the buildings became the plaza, an outdoor living space, which also served as the theater for religious ceremonies. Pueblo culture as it is expressed in dance, architecture, pottery, and weaving is a cohesive whole that always shows a reverence for nature and natural materials but is also a celebration of the human aesthetic. Geometry and line are expressed in organic colors. The joyous hand of the artist who interprets the beauty of nature is always evident. This Pueblo sense of the wholeness of life continues to be the foundation of art and architecture in Santa Fe.

Old village, Acoma Mesa, New Mexico

NAVAJO HERITAGE

Navajo pitch-covered basket water jars

Navajo pictographs, Canyon de Chelly National Monument, Arizona

Navajo blanket (1860s)

Navajo bracelets

The Anasazi were not the only wanderers roaming the Southwest during the thirteenth century. As early as the twelfth century, small bands of nomads were arriving from the north and northwest. The Zuni called these people *apache,* which means "enemy." From the Anasazi the newcomers learned to farm and wear clothes, so they became known as the "apaches who plant fields," or the *navaju.* They settled in the Four Corners area where New Mexico, Arizona, Colorado, and Utah meet. The Anasazi had abandoned this area, but the Navajo claimed the arid, dramatically beautiful land as their home.

The Navajo population is now over 200,000 people, and the tribe controls an area larger than the state of West Virginia. Although these people do not share all of the centuries' long history of the other southwestern tribes, Navajo has long been a dominant Indian culture in the Southwest. The Navajos seem to have a genius for assimilation, and it has served them well. From the Spanish colonists and the Pueblos they learned jewelry making and weaving. From the Spanish colonists they stole horses and became fearless and expert horsemen. Spanish settlers also brought sheep to the New World, and Navajos quickly developed large flocks. They learned to spin and dye the wool with natural colors, and their woven textiles are among the finest in the world. Navajo weaving, as well as the other crafts at which people from the tribe excel, is a fundamental component of Santa Fe design.

Betatakin cliff dwellings, Navajo National Monument, Arizona

St. Francis de Assisi Mission Church (front), Ranchos de Taos

St. Francis de Assisi Mission Church (back), Ranchos de Taos

SPANISH CONQUEST

Not long after the Spanish toppled the mighty empire of the Aztecs, rumors about the Seven Cities of Gold began to circulate among the soldiers and their commanders. In 1540 Francisco Vasquez de Coronado set out to find this vast treasure and claim it for the Spanish crown. Coronado and his men traveled north until they came to the Rio Grande pueblos, which they searched in vain for any sign of gold. After two years the Spanish soldiers returned to Mexico. Coronado's failure dampened Spain's interest in the northern frontier, but after hearing about the large heathen population, members of the Roman Catholic clergy insisted that an effort be made to convert the Pueblos to Christianity. In 1598 Juan de Oñate secured a royal warrant to colonize the province of Nuevo México.

Oñate initially set up camp at a site near Española, but in 1609 he moved his men to what he hoped would be a better location and founded Santa Fe, which remained the provincial capital throughout the Spanish colonial period. From the beginning, Santa Fe was laid out like a European city with a central plaza. The governor's residence, soldiers' quarters, and churches were built around the plaza, but the rest of the village developed haphazardly with houses built along cattle paths and arroyos, or stream beds.

The Franciscan Order of Friars was charged with christianizing the 20,000 Pueblos, as well as the neighboring Navajo, Apache, and Comanche tribes. The Franciscans expected to accomplish this conversion by forcing the Indians to build mission churches. The crown gave each friar ten axes, three adzes, three spades, ten hoes, one medium-sized saw, one chisel, two augers, and one wood plane. He also received a large latch for the church door, two small locks, a dozen hinges, and 6,000 nails of various sizes. These were the first metal tools and hardware the Indians had seen.

Because women and children traditionally built walls, it is likely that they built the mission churches, using pulleys engineered by the friar to erect the massive four-foot-thick walls. The friars also introduced the use of adobe bricks, which allowed thicker and taller walls than Pueblo construction techniques. The Pueblo men, whose traditional tasks were

Mission church and gate, Picuris Pueblo, New Mexico

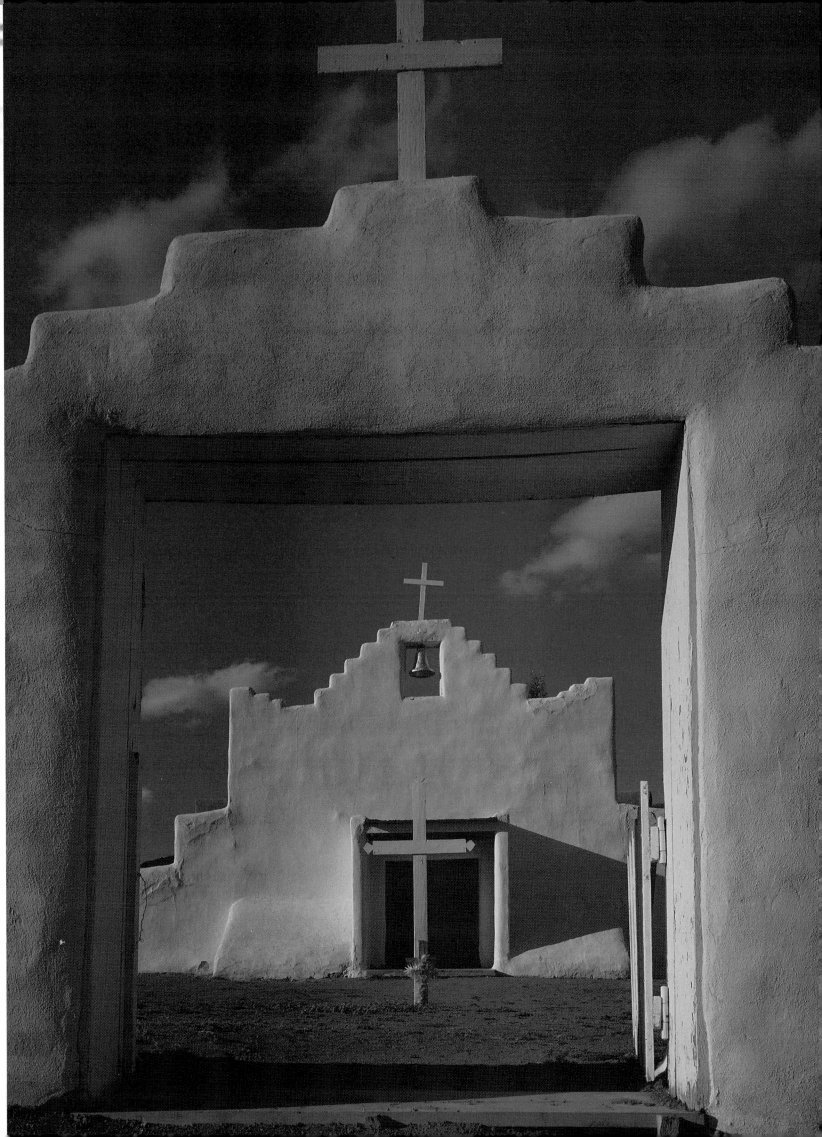

Mission church ruin, Pecos, New Mexico

Statue of La Conquistadora, patroness of New Mexico, St. Francis Cathedral, Santa Fe

San Miguel Mission Church, Santa Fe

hunting, spinning, and weaving, became carpenters and fashioned the woodwork for the new churches.

Glass and planed boards were almost impossible to obtain, so there are only a few small openings for windows and doors in the walls of mission churches. Buttresses, parapets, and bell towers rise from an almost unbroken mass. This makes the churches, which dwarf the Indian villages because of their European scale, seem even larger than they actually are.

Nuevo México

The colonization of the northern province ended abruptly in 1680, when the Pueblos revolted and forced the Spanish to retreat to El Paso, three hundred miles south of Santa Fe. The leader of the rebellion was a San Juan Pueblo warrior known as Popé. Pueblos burned and razed many missions, and plundered the village of Santa Fe. But their valiant efforts to rid their land of its Spanish conquerors ended 12 years later when Diego de Vargas led an expeditionary force back to Nuevo México and began to rebuild the missions.

During the eighteenth century, Spanish colonists in New Mexico were isolated from the rest of the world. Supply caravans from Mexico were rare and unpredictable. Shipments were often lost, stolen, or destroyed by natural disasters, and the exorbitant expense of transporting goods overland limited the kinds of things that were imported. The colonists quickly learned to make do with what was available and to copy the architecture, dress, and food of the native population.

Spanish houses were built around a central *plazuela*. The doors and windows faced inward. Outside walls had few openings, and access into the courtyard was secured by gates. When an attack by Apaches, Comanches, or Navajos seemed likely, grazing animals could be herded into the *plazuela*. As a family grew, rooms were added onto the main house in single file to form an *L* or *U* shape. Animal pens and corrals, stables, and granaries completed the family compound.

Some ranch buildings were made of rubble masonry or notched logs, but most were made of adobe bricks. Making bricks requires clay, sand, silt, straw, water, bright sunlight, and hard work. The raw ingredients are mixed into a thick paste, and straw is added as a binder. The thick mud is poured into wooden, rectangular forms and dried in the sun for two or three days.

The bricks, which weigh 50 to 60 pounds each, are then stacked for final curing.

While the Pueblos built their adobe houses directly on the ground, the Spanish laid two or three courses of rough stones as a foundation for adobe brick walls. The outside walls of an adobe house are smoothed with mud plaster. Depending on weather, plastering must be repeated every two or three years. Interior walls were also plastered with mud. But inside finer pastes of colored mud were carefully applied with a piece of sheepskin. Walls might be white sparkling with flecks of mica, yellow ocher, cocoa brown, salmon, terra-cotta, or even light green.

Pueblo builders did not use wooden corbels or doors, but the Spanish colonists, who had metal woodworking tools, relied on corbels to support roof beams and evenly distribute the weight of the roof. Corbels, which are called *zapatas* in Spanish, were often cut in elaborate scroll or zigzag shapes and carved with rosettes, notches, stars, and other embellishments. During the eighteenth century only wealthy Spanish colonists could afford wooden doors and gates. Most people still covered the entrances to their houses with animal hides. The opening in the wall around a Spanish family compound is called a *zaguan*. These openings were secured by a heavy, wooden double door called a *portón*. Metal hinges were rare, so the *portón* revolved on rounded wooden pegs installed in sockets dug out of the lintels.

The Spanish colonists also added *portales,* or porches, to their adobe buildings. Squared timbers supporting carved *zapatas* and heavy lintels were roofed with *vigas* and *latillas* to make a porch or covered walkway. The block-long colonnade of the Palace of Governors in Santa Fe was built in the early eighteenth century.

The fireplace is another important Spanish contribution to adobe architecture. In the pueblos smoke from the fire pit escaped through an opening in the roof, which was also the entrance to the room. The Spanish colonists placed the hearth in one corner of the room. A large room would have two fireplaces placed in opposite corners. These fireplaces were small, with shallow fireboxes and elliptical openings. Firewood was leaned vertically against the back wall of the firebox.

The Indians adopted some of the Spanish adaptations of their historic build-

Rancho de las Golondrinas, La Cienega, New Mexico

Interior mission church, Trampas, New Mexico

Mission church, Chimayo, New Mexico

ing techniques. These eighteenth century refinements of traditional Pueblo architecture created rooms that were more comfortable. Low earthen benches, or *bancos,* built into the walls provided seating. Adobe brick walls could accommodate larger window openings and wooden doors. Hearths and fireplaces were built in the corners of rooms. Interior walls were whitewashed with gypsum (gesso), or plastered in two colors with white plaster above and a dark earthen band, or dado, encircling the room three or four feet above the floor. During this time the plaza between the apartment houses took on new importance as the stage for ceremonial dances. Terraces on the various levels of the pueblos were built to serve as communal spaces and used to dry chiles, corn, and fruit. People met on the terraces to talk and set up their looms.

Mission church, Trampas

27

Cochiti-style silla *(chair)*

Trastero

Wrought-iron grille, Cerrillos, New Mexico

Colonial Crafts

The Spanish introduced furniture to New Mexico. The Pueblos had always sat on the ground, in the lap of Mother Earth. But under the direction of Spanish craftsmen, Pueblo men became capable cabinetmakers. Pecos Pueblo was the major woodworking center during the seventeenth century. The chairs, tables, and chests produced there were highly valued, and owning furniture was considered a mark of wealth and high social status.

Furniture was so valuable partly because it was so difficult to make. Pine trees had to be felled by ax or with a two-handed Spanish bucksaw, or *sierra*. Crude boards were made from rough timber with axes, adzes, and handsaws. Lumber had to be planed by hand, so Spanish colonial furniture tends to be crude and massive. Because nails were scarce, *carpinteros* used mortise-and-tenon joinery to construct furniture. The exposed wooden tenon, which passes completely through the board into which the mortise is cut, often became a distinctive decorative feature.

The most common piece of colonial furniture is the *caja,* or chest, which was used to store clothing and valuables under lock and key. The simplest chests were made by joining four boards and attaching a top and bottom with pegs or metal hinges. Other *cajas* were built on legs. While the construction of colonial chests is straightforward, many were elaborately decorated with carved or painted designs or pictures. Rosettes, pomegranates, lions, and crosses, which were popular artistic conventions in Spain during the Middle Ages, were repeated and reinterpreted by New Mexican craftsmen. In the area around Santa Cruz and Taos, chests were chip carved in Moorish-style designs.

Tables were usually made for use in churches, as were armchairs, which were known as priest's chairs. Only wealthy families, clergy, and government officials could afford chairs and benches, and most people sat on *bancos* or on the hard-packed earth floor. Beds were unknown in New Mexico until the late nineteenth century. The colonists slept on wool sacks and sheep pelts. During the day the sacks were used as floor cushions, and the pelts were suspended from the ceiling.

The lack of diversity in colonial furniture is made up for by the richness of the designs of *trasteros,* or cupboards, which in the eighteenth century became the principal piece of furniture in many New Mexican homes. Some of these huge, upright cabinets are more than seven feet high, and the *carpinteros* who built them imbued their work with the full measure of their skill and creativity.

Along with carpentry, Spanish colonists also introduced metalwork to the Southwest. Blacksmiths working in small family workshops made tools, hardware, and horseshoes. Tinsmiths produced candelabra and wall sconces. Silversmiths made delicate filigree jewelry for women and stamped, engraved, or cast silver pieces for *charros* (cowboys) and their horses. Navajos and Pueblos learned silversmithing from Spanish jewelers, adapting Hispanic designs and techniques to make their own unique silver and turquoise jewelry.

The Spanish colonists were devoted to their church, and *santos* (painted and sculpted images of saints) stood in prominent places in almost every home. Family shrines held *bultos* (figurines) and *retablos* (painted panels) that were made by master artists and their apprentices or by family members. Eighteenth century masters, such as Molleno and José Rafael Aragón, developed an unmistakable style by distorting facial features to express sorrow and grief. Even in the ghastly image of Death as a skeleton riding in a cart, the deep faith of these artists is apparent. The grim reaper is intended to remind the faithful of the transitory nature of their earthly existence and their hope for salvation.

Before Spanish colonization Indian weavers had depended on cultivated cotton fiber. But by the seventeenth century, they had begun to use wool, which the Spanish colonists had introduced. Spanish weavers worked on large, horizontal wooden shuttle looms, making cloth for clothing; heavier, patterned Rio Grande blankets; and *jergas,* or rugs. Navajo looms were much simpler and stood upright; they were used to make blankets.

Coined money was rare on the frontier, so most transactions were barter. Annual trade fairs were held at Pecos and Taos Pueblos. Comanches and Apaches brought buffalo meat and tanned hides and robes. Pueblos traded pottery, clothing, corn, and baskets. The Spanish colonists bartered with Rio Grande blankets and metal tools and knives. Horses and captured Indian slaves also changed hands. This cross-cultural exchange of goods on which colonial life depended has evolved through the centuries into the eclecticism of what is known today as Santa Fe design, a rich and complex blend of European and native American styles.

Rio Grande blanket

Navajo silver necklace

Apache buckskin shirt

Tinwork cross made in Rio Abajo Workshop

Rain-cloud design window, Tesuque Pueblo, New Mexico

MEXICAN COLONY

The cultural and economic isolation that helped shape the unique culture of New Mexico suddenly ended in 1821. Mexico, now independent from Spain, took over the remote northern province and opened it to trade with its eastern neighbor, the United States. William Becknell was the first trader to arrive from Missouri. He had set out to trade with the Comanches and other Rocky Mountain tribes, but changed his plans and arrived in Santa Fe with a limited supply of cloth and metal tools. Becknell realized an extraordinary profit on the goods he sold in Santa Fe and quickly established a trade route from Independence, Missouri, to Santa Fe.

From early spring until late fall, caravans of covered wagons pulled into New Mexico villages, where they were greeted by clanging church bells and throngs of excited people hoping to exchange meat, cheese, and garden vegetables for the goods the Americans had to offer. The most coveted items were farm tools, such as hoes, plows, and sickles; carpenters' tools, such as planes, saws, axes, and hammers; and building materials, such as nails, screws, padlocks, and window panes. The traders also did a brisk business in calico, European textiles, thimbles, needles, coffee pots, mirrors, combs, perfume, bowls, plates, clocks, coffee, and liquor.

Carved single-panel shutters, Santa Fe

Synopco Compound, Santa Fe

Loretto Chapel, Santa Fe

Carved shell design above window, Albuquerque, New Mexico

From Santa Fe some traders went south to Mexico following the Camino Real. Since there were only 30,000 people living in New Mexico in the 1820s, the larger Mexican market, particularly Chihuahua, attracted more and more traders from the United States, with Santa Fe becoming the hub for this burgeoning international trade. Prosperity came to the town, and several of the wealthiest traders built impressive haciendas nearby.

Severino Martínez constructed a 12-room house in Taos in 1825. *Portales* extend along the front and inner courtyard of the Martínez mansion, but there are no windows in the outside walls of this fortresslike structure. The Martínez hacienda marks the passing of an era in New Mexico. Built to withstand Indian attack and serve the Chihuahua trade, the house is simply a basic frontier dwelling built on a grand scale. The large, almost medieval hacienda contrasts sharply with buildings built only a few decades later. These structures, such as the Romanesque Cathedral of St. Francis built in 1869 under the direction the first archbishop of Santa Fe, Juan Bautista Lamy, reflect the cosmopolitan aspect of life in New Mexico that quickly developed through increased trade with the United States. The organic style of the Martínez hacienda, which combines Pueblo and Spanish architecture, was soon eclipsed by the formal style introduced by the Americans.

Altar, Loretto Chapel, Santa Fe

31

Depot and Quarter-Master's Office (September 1866), Fort Union

Wagon ruts, Fort Union National Monument, New Mexico

Adobe walls of the machine shops, Fort Union National Monument

Adobe wall and territorial-style doorway, Isleta, New Mexico

AMERICAN TERRITORY

The Santa Fe Trail prepared the way for the conquest of New Mexico by the United States Army in the summer of 1846. Earlier that year Brigadier General Stephen Watts Kearny had set out from Fort Leavenworth, Kansas, under orders from President James K. Polk to conquer northern California. He was also ordered to seize Santa Fe. Kearny took Santa Fe without a fight, but his action set off the Mexican War, which resulted in the United States annexing all of the Southwest and California.

Under U.S. authority trade along the Santa Fe Trail increased, but hostile Indians on the Great Plains continued to threaten trade caravans. In 1851 the army built Fort Union in northeastern New Mexico. The garrison stationed there was charged with protecting the trade routes. Traffic along the Santa Fe Trail continued to increase, and in 1862 the army decided to expand and rebuild Fort Union. The architect for the new buildings favored the Greek revival style, which had been out of fashion on the East Coast for more than 40 years. This style was still popular on the frontier, where it was often used for town halls and courthouses. Classical Greek architectural elements could be adapted to many different sizes of buildings, and the formal proportions implied a sense of order, elegance, and grandeur.

At Fort Union, Greek revival elements were blended with adobe construction techniques in what has become known as the territorial style. Squat mud-brick structures have pedimental wooden window casings with double-hung sash windows. The glass panes are small—only 9 inches square—because they had to endure a 700-mile journey in a covered wagon. Windows also flank central doorways, which are much larger than the entrances to Spanish and Indian dwellings. The entire building sits on a stone masonry foundation, which protects it from ground moisture. A handsome wooden porch is made of square timbers with applied trim molding to form simple classical columns with capitals and bases.

The officers' quarters at Fort Union were the first formally planned houses in New Mexico. In these buildings paired front and rear rooms flank a central hallway. One front room

Adobe walls, Fort Union National Monument, New Mexico

Victorian house, Silver City, New Mexico

Territorial window molding, Las Vegas, New Mexico

Victorian interior, Santa Fe

served as a parlor, the other as a master bedroom. The children's bedroom and a kitchen-dining room occupied the back of the house. The large central hallway, some of which were 14 feet wide, was perfect for dancing and parties.

In addition to a new architectural style, the army introduced new construction techniques and materials, which greatly improved the permanence and comfort of adobe buildings. Many Americans who visited New Mexico recorded their disdain for adobe homes in their journals and diaries. But until the railroad arrived, small window panes and floorboards were the only improvements on Pueblo interiors that most settlers could afford. The army built the first brick kiln in New Mexico and began to quarry for lime to make mortar and exterior plaster. To give buildings a classical look, wet plaster was often scored with a sharp tool to make it look like cut-stone masonry. The army imported sheets of tin and zinc for roofs, and it was not long until gable and ridge tin roofs had replaced roofs covered with handmade wooden shingles. In structures with flat roofs, muslin was stretched across ceiling vigas and treated with flour paste to form a waterproof membrane between the soggy, earthen roof and the interior.

Territorial Haciendas
Between 1850 and 1880 many fortunes were made on the New Mexican frontier. Traders, sheep and cattle ranchers, suppliers of the military posts, and merchants prospered. These men and their families built grand haciendas that magnificently express their wealth, style, and ambition. The great territorial mansions feature a dramatic extension of rooms upward to two stories of adobe. The house built for José Albino Baca in Las Vegas, New Mexico, even has a third, attic story. The front facade of these haciendas often had double *portales* of symmetrically spaced posts that were capped by a simple gable roof. The overall effect was classically elegant, not unlike Southern antebellum plantation houses.

Like many other territorial haciendas, Samuel Watrous's house was built on a huge ranch near the Santa Fe Trail. Watrous made big money supplying cattle and grain to the army at Fort Union, and over time, his house grew to 26 rooms surrounding a courtyard. Unlike colonial houses in which most rooms served many functions, the Watrous home has separate parlors and bedrooms. Like houses back East, this hacienda has fireplaces located in the middle of walls rather than in the corners. Elaborate Greek revival mantelpieces frame otherwise simple, elliptical adobe hearths. Another departure from colonial architecture is a long exterior face broken by windows, shutters, and pedimented lintels similar to those on the officers' quarters at Fort Union.

One of the major distinguishing features of the territorial style is the pedimental lintel, which is a triangular piece of wooden trim used to crown windows and doorways. The amount of carved molding applied to the lintel implied the wealth and status of the owner in much the same way that elaborately carved corbels had been a status symbol during the colonial period. In addition to adding lintels, territorial architecture also abandoned corbels in favor of simple molded trim capitals and bases.

Railroad Era

On July 4, 1879, hundreds of cheering New Mexicans greeted a flag-draped Baldwin engine of the Atchison, Topeka and Santa Fe Railroad as it pulled into Las Vegas, sixty miles northeast of Santa Fe. Ironically, the Santa Fe Railroad bypassed Santa Fe on its way west to Albuquerque. The closest stop was Lamy, a supply depot, eighteen miles south of Santa Fe. Within a year the Denver and Rio Grande Railroad supplied Santa Fe with rail service, but the city was quickly eclipsed by Albuquerque and Las Vegas, which had larger populations and stronger economies.

The railroad brought the architectural styles of the Victorian era to New Mexico. Shimmering, shingled Queen Anne homes; stately Italianate villas; picturesque Gothic revival manors; and graceful Second Empire mansions were built next to adobe houses that must have seemed shabby by comparison. The trains brought cast-iron columns, pressed metal ornamental window hoods, all kinds and colors of brick, large panes of glass, shingles, many colors of paint, wallpaper, hardwood flooring, milled lumber, wooden molding, factory-built doors, porcelain washbasins, bathtubs, brass hardware, chandeliers, curtains, and carpets. Colors, patterns, and textures that had never before been seen in Santa Fe were suddenly accessible to almost everyone. Many adobe interiors were simply Victorianized by covering every exposed surface with carpets, wallpaper, cloth, wooden molding and paneling, and stamped metal ceilings. Packed earth floors were planked over. Carved wooden mantels were fitted onto adobe fire-

Victorian frame and stucco mansion, Las Vegas, New Mexico

Parlor, Victorian house, Santa Fe

Atchison, Topeka and Santa Fe Railroad depot (built 1898), Las Vegas

Church, Madrid, New Mexico

Case Trading Post, Wheelwright Museum, Santa Fe

places. Victorian bric-a-brac and mass-produced furniture replaced handmade objects in many Santa Fe homes.

To correspond with the new look in interiors, streets were surveyed, broadened, and organized on a grid. Parks were laid out symmetrically with neat rows of trees, and house lots began to be fenced in. Las Vegas and Albuquerque soon had entire blocks of wood-frame, brick, and stone buildings in the new American style. Santa Fe did not succumb as completely to the charms of Victorian architecture. As early as 1883 concerned citizens of Santa Fe organized to save the old San Miguel Church from destruction. But there was no holding back the modern world. Gas lights were introduced in Santa Fe in 1880; electricity followed in 1891. By the turn of the century, fired bricks had replaced adobe as the basic building material.

In Santa Fe many builders opted to graft Victorian wooden architectural elements onto adobe houses. Italianate, Queen Anne, and Classical porches became a symbol of status. Fancy milled columns, bracketed cornices, friezes, and window hoods could be ordered through catalogs and bought locally. But in remote villages local carpenters often fabricated their own versions of Victorian gingerbread. These folk adobe Victorian houses continue to delight us with their charm and whimsy.

Home on the Range

When many Americans took up their *manifest destiny* and moved West, they encountered nomadic Indian tribes and vast open spaces. The culture and way of life that the settlers brought with them essentially met with no challenge or resistance. But in New Mexico the Americans encountered entrenched Indian and European cultures. The Pueblo Indians were not nomads, and they had already endured three centuries of the white man's presence in their homeland. Unlike other Indians, they could not attempt to move out of the Americans' way. To a greater extent than elsewhere, American settlers in New Mexico learned to live on the land in the ways the Indians had. Many Americans also took up the ways of the *vaqueros,* or Spanish cowboys.

With the building of army posts at Fort Union, Fort Stanton, and Fort Sumner in eastern New Mexico, settlers and land speculators began to move into the vast grasslands of the Great Plains. Land in Texas was rapidly becoming fenced in, and cattlemen bought large tracts of grazing land in New Mexico

Adobe house with gable roof, Las Vegas

at very low prices. By 1875 more than 300,000 head of cattle roamed the prairie nourished by Rio Pecos. Cattle drives roared through the land. Rodeos brought Anglo, Hispanic, and Navajo cowboys together to compete for prize money and highly prized silver championship belt buckles.

While the railroads were transforming New Mexican cities and towns into facsimiles of Victorian urban centers anywhere else in the United States, a unique cowboy aesthetic was developing on the plains. The Victorian style was primarily refined and cosmopolitan and the New Mexican ranch style was rough and rustic, but the two styles are often interwoven inside a ranch house. Ranch structures were simple but sturdy buildings made of adobe, ledge sandstone, or logs, whichever material happened to be available on the ranch. Massive stone fireplaces; plank floors and walls (sometimes adorned with the owner's and neighbors' brands burned in); and high, pitched and raftered ceilings are common features of ranch houses. Their interiors are casually eclectic. Solid wooden furniture, probably bought from one of the railroad mercantile companies, anchors the large sitting room. Beveled mirrored Victorian buffets, mission revival rocking chairs, and worn Navajo rugs add to the rich mix. Heavy handforged pokers and andirons stand on the hearth. A huge elk head hangs over the mantel. Pueblo pots and paintings by cowboy artists complete the scene.

Territorial portales, *Sena Plaza, Santa Fe*

Sandstone ranch building

HISTORIC REVIVALS

Facade KiMo Theatre, Albuquerque, New Mexico

Buffalo-skull lights, balcony, KiMo Theatre

Ornament above second story windows, KiMo Theatre

New Mexico became a state in 1912, and many citizens were pleased to be able to put the Spanish and Mexican colonial past behind them. But in Santa Fe some people had begun to feel differently about their city's past. They did not want to lose their unique heritage by letting Santa Fe become just another American town. In 1909 the Archaeological Society took one of the first steps toward preserving Santa Fe's rich past when society members decided to create a new museum to house the School of American Archaeology. They decided to remodel the old governor's palace on the plaza and use it for the museum. The territorial porch was removed, and the palace was restored to its colonial appearance. This restoration and the museum itself sparked a new and ever-growing interest in the rich architectural history of Santa Fe.

During the decade before 1920, archaeologists and artists from the East Coast converged on Santa Fe and Taos, 75 miles to the north. Archaeologists excavated many important Pueblo ruins. Designers and architects turned to the Indian and colonial past for inspiration for their work, and several important shows of paintings of Indians in their native surroundings were mounted at the new museum.

Archaeology in New Mexico has made more than a thousand years of history accessible to twentieth century designers, so naturally, many different points of view on what is authentically and appropriately Santa Fe style have developed. Some of the first buildings designed to reflect Pueblo architecture were built at the University of New Mexico in 1910. But the 1914 Panama California Exposition in San Diego was a major turning point for this style of architecture. Isaac Hamilton Rapp and his brother William Morris Rapp were awarded the commission to design the New Mexico Pavilion. The Rapps had been an important regional architectural firm since 1890. In addition to many major buildings in Las Vegas and Santa Fe, they designed the territorial capitol buildings and the governor's mansion. I.H. Rapp incorporated Pueblo motifs into his design for the pavilion, which he later revised for the Santa Fe Museum of Fine Arts. The design adapts the mission church facades of Acoma and Laguna Pueblos in a series of gal-

Wrought-iron crane railing, lobby, KiMo Theatre

La Fonda Hotel, Santa Fe

Dining room, Los Poblanos, John Gaw Meem, architect. Photograph by Laura Gilpin, 1939

Library, Los Poblanos. Photograph by Laura Gilpin, 1939

leries organized around a central *plazuela,* or courtyard. Massive carved wooden roof beams and corbels, projecting *vigas,* terraced half walls, and balconies are brought together to create this eclectic masterpiece. The building is furnished with chairs and tables designed by archaeologist Jesse Nusbaum, who based his designs on Spanish colonial furniture.

Houses as well as public buildings were designed in the Santa Fe style. Sylvanus Morley reworked an old adobe house in 1910. Designer Carlos Vierra's 1916 house is a fully realized Pueblo revival mansion. Vierra was so enthusiastic about this design style that he sold lots along Buena Vista Loma only to builders who were planning to build Pueblo revival cottages on the property.

By 1912 Santa Fe had its first appointed city planning board. The board's recommendations included renaming such streets as College Avenue and Railroad Avenue with appropriate Spanish names and recognizing certain buildings and streets as historic sites. They also wanted all new buildings to be built in the Pueblo revival style so that they would look old. None of these recommendations became official policy, but many builders and developers attempted to go along with the board's suggestions. Although Santa Fe did not enact a historic preservation ordinance until 1957, the community was one of the first in the United States to become interested in historic preservation. Starting in 1922 one group of volunteers attempted to restore the colonial mission churches that had badly deteriorated. Under the leadership of Anne Evans, they worked on one church each summer, reroofing the naves and replastering crumbling adobe walls.

During the 1920s several landmarks of Santa Fe style were built: the La Fonda Hotel, Santa Fe's Federal Building, and the KiMo Theatre. While Art Deco was attracting attention throughout the world, Santa Fe designers were developing a style based on ancient stylistic traditions. Their work fit right in with the interest in primitive motifs that was generated by Picasso and other cubist painters whose work refers directly to African tribal art.

In New Mexico artists and designers had direct access to the primitive past. Artifacts were not shut up in museums, they were in everyday use at Taos and other pueblos. Ancient sites, as well as dramatic natural settings, could easily be reached by car. The painter Georgia O'Keeffe is the best known artist who came to New Mexico in the 1930s, but Andrew Dasburg, John Marin, Edward Hopper, and Marsden Hartley also explored Southwestern themes in their work. The extraordinary light and vast open skies as well as the ancient cultures also attracted photographers to New Mexico. Ansel Adams, Laura Gilpin, Edward Weston, and Paul Strand worked here. These artists along with many others not only created a legacy of stunningly beautiful images of the Southwest, but they also had a major impact on historic preservation. The Santa Fe arts colony became the city's most effective political lobbying group and was responsible for changing the preservation of Santa Fe architecture from a sentimental dream into a well-financed campaign.

During the 1930s the nature of Santa Fe design was evolving. At the beginning of the Pueblo revival, some designers, such as Carlos Vierra and Sylvanus Morley, had advocated an archaeological approach to building that incorporated decorative details based on historic Pueblo structures. Rapp had been another major design influence. His interpretations of Santa Fe design featured an interplay of picturesque facades loosely based on historical examples of mission churches. Santa Fe architect John Gaw Meem managed to incorporate both the archaeological and the picturesque points of view and to fuse them into well-balanced buildings. In his work he found inspiration not only in the Pueblo tradition and the mission revival but also in the territorial style. From modest, meticulously crafted residences to the monumental Zimmerman library on the Albuquerque campus of the University of New Mexico, Meem interpreted his version of Santa Fe design in a wide variety of buildings. By incorporating modern construction materials, such as hollow clay building tiles and decorative cast concrete details, Meem made this kind of architecture less expensive and more durable.

Pueblo revival house, Santa Fe

Mabel Dodge Luhan's house, Taos

West facade, Zimmerman Library, University of New Mexico

La Posada, Albuquerque

Dining room, Santa Fe

During the years before the Depression, the movement to revive historic architecture encouraged a renewed interest in Southwest arts and crafts. The Santa Fe Indian Market was first held in 1922. Today the annual event attracts more than 100,000 visitors. Traditional Spanish crafts were also revived. Ceramicist Frank Applegate recognized the integrity and intrinsic beauty of the religious art of New Mexico, and he was influential in setting up the Spanish Colonial Arts Society, which also holds an annual market.

When the Depression left many people in Santa Fe without work, Leonora Curtin and members of the Spanish Colonial Arts Society persuaded state officials to begin a training program in traditional Hispanic arts and crafts. Vocational schools were set up throughout northern New Mexico. The programs offered courses in furniture making, spinning and dyeing, weaving, tanning and leatherwork, and wood carving. Under the direction of Bill Lumpkins, apprentices carefully measured and made shop drawings of outstanding examples of colonial furniture. Even though many Hispanic craftsman studied these drawings, the furniture they built, based on historic prototypes, has its own distinctive style and appeal. The proportions are much more massive, and the use of modern woodworking tools is evident.

The years following World War II brought many changes to Santa Fe architecture. During the 1950s and 1960s schools, commercial buildings, fast-food restaurants, and even tract houses were designed in earth-colored stucco with projecting vigas. The remaining American storefronts on the plaza were given a Southwestern look, and John Gaw Meem designed *portales* for three sides of the plaza, so it now looks older and more unified.

After 1965 Santa Fe architecture took a new departure from the romantic styles of the Pueblo and colonial revivals. The new Santa Fe Opera by McHugh and Kidder, and Antoine Predock's La Luz Condominiums in Albuquerque use the adobe vernacular to express streamlined, modernist forms. The building lines are no longer picturesque but angular, straight, and regular. Both buildings introduce a dynamic relationship between construction and landscape, between outside and inside. These architects have moved away from Meem's romantic vision. A building's form and relationship to its site are more important to the design than ornament and historical reference.

In addition to innovative designs by local architects, Santa Fe design today has also been shaped by Post-Modernism. For much of the twentieth century, the international style dominated residential design. This style resulted from attempts by Le Corbusier and the Bauhaus school to rid architecture and interior design of frivolous and decadent details. But in the United States, the style became a tyranny of rigid geometry; stark, white interiors; and manufactured furniture made of chrome, glass, and plastic. Post-Modernism encourages a reinvestigation of traditional historic styles and motifs. But the designer is free to reformulate them in a new, idiosyncratic way, juxtaposing traditional and industrial materials and employing harmonies and proportions previously limited by the accepted rules of design.

After the austerity of the international style, people are hungry for color, texture, hand-rubbed finishes, and hand-made objects with some kind of symbolic meaning. Santa Fe design has all this and more. Old Spanish furniture is valued for signs of wear, and fading paint increases its value in the showroom. Designers have learned to scratch, stain, wax, and varnish to produce old-looking tables and chairs. Plaster is textured to mimic adobe, and hand-glazed tiles are set in place around hot tubs and porcelain sinks.

You might say that we have come full circle. A thousand years ago, the Anasazi enjoyed a natural, all-encompassing way of life. By desire and design, this way of life has returned. Santa Fe style is more than the picturesque look of an adobe-colored house against the landscape. It is more than a carefully arranged room filled with handcrafted pottery, weaving, and furniture. It surpasses the rugged appeal of leather and denim clothing, and it satisfies more than zesty enchiladas and a cool margarita. Above all, Santa Fe design is a celebration of the gifts of nature to a people lucky enough to live in the ancient Anasazi homeland.

Santa Fe Opera

Architect's model for Pottery House by Frank Lloyd Wright

Plaza and Palace of the Governors, Santa Fe

SANTA FE
ARCHITECTURE

Santa Fe architecture was exemplified by the work of John Gaw Meem from 1930 until the mid-1960s, but his most important commissions were realized before 1940. Meem successfully adapted the predominant themes of Pueblo adobe architecture to twentieth century expectations for comfort and convenience. The architect was a master of spatial organization and decorative detail, and his work is easily recognized by the way in which Meem integrated architectural design elements, including corbels, wrought iron, light fixtures, paneled doors, and furniture, into a cohesive and beautiful whole. His work continues to be a source of inspiration for today's Southwestern architects, but since the mid-1960s, Santa Fe design has moved away from Meem's revival style to include a wide range of inventive design themes.

Two breakthrough projects mark the beginning of contemporary Santa Fe architectural design. The Santa Fe Opera House (1966–67), designed by McHugh, Kidder, demonstrated the sculptural potential of adobe architecture, and La Luz Condominiums in Albuquerque (1968), designed by Antoine Predock, blended a modernist approach to Southwestern house design with a Pueblo sensitivity for setting.

Most Santa Fe designers working today embrace a post-modern attitude in their residential plans, allowing them to investigate historic design styles in search of elements, plans, and facade elevations. Never before have all New Mexico building styles—Pueblo, Spanish colonial, territorial, and Victorian—been expressed simultaneously. While today's architects borrow from past traditions, they are not bound by the rules of those traditions. Just as styles are freely mixed, certain traditions are being expanded and changed as architects find new design solutions.

Some Santa Fe designers are the vanguard of an international adobe style, which borrows from North African and Mediterranean architecture as well as Native American sources. But the rich legacy of purely Southwestern adobe architecture continues to inspire other architects to pursue a strongly regional style. New building technologies and design sensibilites have helped Santa Fe design break free from the comfortable quaintness that used to categorize many expressions of the style, but it is the way in which many of today's architects approach their work with a sculptor's sense of form and a painter's sense of color that has radically transformed Santa Fe design.

Right: The interplay of dyed stuccos, square openings, circular lamps, and glass-block sidelights creates a fusion of Pueblo form and Art Deco ornamentation.

Left: The center for Non-Invasive Diagnosis on the campus of the University of New Mexico in Albuquerque elaborates the Pueblo revival aesthetic of the campus, which was developed largely under the guidance of John Gaw Meem.

Right: This reinterpretation of Pueblo revival architecture employs industrial materials with pleasing visual effects. The lines of the building are hard, but they harmonize with the landscape and other architectural elements, such as the long steel I beam that helps fashion the pergola.

Right: This high wall with its imposing entrance gate is a recent version of a standard Spanish colonial design that is found throughout Mexico and the Southwest. The entrance to this contemporary hacienda is handsomely detailed with a pair of weathered gates flanked on one side by a terra-cotta lamp and on the other by painted tile house numbers.

Left: In the Los Ranchos Community Center, Westwork Architects introduces bold, graphic design to exterior stucco ornamentation. As in many post-modern buildings, the entrances are exaggerated and loosely modeled on historical precedents. The large garage doors boast pedimental lintels that were common during New Mexico's territorial period, and the main entrance has a classical profile.

Left: Streamlined sculptural walls, free of extraneous ornament, create a pleasing balance between vertical thrust and horizontal expansion. These cylindrical rooms also make direct reference to Anasazi and Pueblo kivas.

Right: This two-story construction of colored earth sits comfortably among the trees. Only a few details—a window, an archway, a small chimney, and a downspout—define the structure and separate it from the landscape.

Above: This house is an architectural counterpoint to the mountains. Southwestern design traditions can be seen in the soft earth colors and horizontal mass, but the house presents the familiar pueblo profile as planes rather than cubes.

Left: When the Santa Fe Opera was built in 1966–67, it was a major departure from traditional adobe architecture. A masterpiece of organic and sculptural expressionism, the open-air opera house embodies an exuberant, soaring spirit, but paradoxically it sits firmly in piñon-clad foothills on the outskirts of the city.

Right: *Los Miradores, a condominium complex, looks very much like a pueblo. Its color and shape harmonize with its site in much the same way Taos Pueblo relates to the landscape around it.*

Above: *This house displays characteristics of fine Pueblo revival architecture: heavy, rounded massing; projecting vigas; undulating roof and parapet profiles; and a uniform skin of earth-colored plaster.*

Below and left: *This modern house, which refers directly to ancient Hohokam and Anasazi dwellings, sits firmly in the rock-strewn Sonoran desert among saguaro and mesquite. The organic and free-flowing adobe structure takes full advantage of its site and seems to grow out of the giant boulders.*

Left: *Pitched roofs with corrugated iron sheathing were first brought to New Mexico by the railroad in 1879. The soggy, earthen flat roofs on adobe houses were quickly modified with wooden gables to support this superior roofing material. This house is derived from the hybrid architectural style that developed.*

Right: *Asymmetrical house plans, complex roof shapes, porches, bay windows, balconies, and sun rooms are typical of Victorian era Queen Anne houses. But the choice of stucco as a building material adds a contemporary Southwestern touch to this home.*

Right: *This streamlined variation of territorial-style architecture is a successful mix of adobe building technique with Greek-revival details. Window frames and the molded cornice provide classical accents; flat roofs and terraced building shapes are standards of adobe structures.*

Above: *This house presents a complex interplay of traditional Pueblo and American-territorial design motifs. But a central gable unifies two flanking wings that are articulated by square windows and a square window grid.*

Above: *A dominant gable roof and earthen-colored stucco unify an intriguing pastiche of historical architectural elements. The Palladian fanlight window in the gable and pedimental window frames on the ground level are classic architectural motifs. But the gingerbread porch evokes the Victorian era.*

53

Left: The entrance courtyard of this house by Westwork Architects presents several geometric and colorful juxtapositions. Like many Spanish colonial haciendas, this house has three wings, but only its shape is traditional; the building materials and design attitudes are completely contemporary.

Right: Abstract planes of chocolate-colored stucco and a startling, undulating ribbon of turquoise wall form a cubist design. The archway terminates in a fountain in the courtyard, and its wavy design suggests the flow of water.

Right: The view of one complete facade of this house shows the way in which the turquoise wall both separates and unites the two halves of the design: One side is clearly a modernist pueblo, while the other is a post-modern cubist fantasy.

Left: The heavy cornice ornament on this face is offset with circular lamps and the downspouts. The wall does not end with a squared off corner but flows into a lovely semicylindrical and curving exterior wall.

55

Left: The cubical form of this house manifests dramatic sculptural integrity and interest because the curving entrance wall balances and unifies the structure.

Above: The gentle, rounded adobe walls of this Pueblo-style house are updated and streamlined by the post-and-lintel porch with a steel shed roof.

Left: Its rounded corner buttresses that flow into the chimneys and scroll back into projecting downspouts give this facade a strong reference to the fortifications of Spanish colonial haciendas.

Left: In New Mexico railroad towns at the beginning of the twentieth century, the California mission style was popular for depots, commercial buildings, and residences. In this Taos home, the encircling terra-cotta roof tiles of the veranda and the corner parapets are trademarks of that design style.

Right: *This house by Westwork Architects is a modernist expression of some of the themes of New Mexico architecture, such as cubical form and a neutral palette of colored stucco. But the harmonious progression of walls that terminates in the multistory house block is somewhat reminiscent of the work of the French architect Le Corbusier.*

Above: *Orange stucco and a natural wood door keep this entrance composition from becoming stark and mechanical. A cylinder, which is half solid and half void, is bisected by a plane with two rectangular openings, so that it seems to be a mysterious stage set.*

Right: *Strict rectangular geometry governs another facade of this house. Concrete columns rise in a rhythmic progression toward a block window tower, which pays homage symbolically to the Sandia Mountains.*

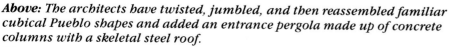

Above: *The architects have twisted, jumbled, and then reassembled familiar cubical Pueblo shapes and added an entrance pergola made up of concrete columns with a skeletal steel roof.*

Right: Projecting roof vigas are a mainstay of Southwestern architecture, but in this house they are grafted onto a Moorish design. Islamic architecture was introduced to New Mexico in 1981 (although certain Spanish colonial motifs originally came from the Moors) by Hasson Fathy through a mosque he designed in Abiquiu.

Left: Squat columns and arches lend a breezy personality to this house, and the neo-Palladian arched windows contribute a sense of rhythm, when modern and classic themes are blended to create a sophisticated Southwestern villa.

Below: The image of a Mediterranean villa is fostered by classically inspired arcades that frame the entrances to this house. The terraced rooftops capped by territorial-style decorative brickwork are echoed in the stepped landscaping.

CASA SANTA FE

From its beginnings in Anasazi and Pueblo cultures, Santa Fe design has expressed an organic warmth with a minimum of clutter. The pueblos had no furnishings, wall hangings, or ornamentation. Their architecture alone made them beautiful places for people to live. The lovely ceiling vigas and earth-surfaced walls and floors were the only design elements in these rooms, but these elements were enhanced with pottery and baskets crafted of natural materials and decorated with organic colors.

Centuries later, Spanish colonists developed their own interiors, tempered by European values but severely restricted by the hardships and isolation of the New Mexico frontier. Like medieval European houses, colonial haciendas contained large, multifunction rooms instead of a series of smaller rooms with special functions, such as kitchens, bedrooms, and parlors. Although the Spanish colonists introduced carpentry and furniture making to New Mexico, the expense of transporting materials or finished furniture forced most colonists to live in sparsely furnished interiors much like those of the Pueblos. But the fireplace, a *nicho* holding the family's *santos,* and perhaps a woven or embroidered wall hanging differentiated a colonial adobe room from a Pueblo home.

The American occupation brought an entirely new domestic standard to New Mexico. Glass windows, floorboards, beds, cupboards, and even a few pianos were brought in by wagons along the Santa Fe Trail. With the coming of the railroad, this trickle of goods increased to a flood, and Santa Fe interiors soon began to look much like rooms in other parts of the country.

The twentieth century turned the dominant trend in Santa Fe design back toward its roots in Pueblo and Spanish interiors. But along with Pueblo revival architecture and colonial revival furniture, a new eclectic style became popular, as traditional Southwestern art objects took their place among American furniture, carpets, and paintings. Today both revival and eclectic interiors are still an important part of Santa Fe design, but there is also a new trend toward minimalist rooms that depend on expansive space and the integrity of adobe architecture for maximum dramatic effect.

A recent trend in Santa Fe design combines Southwestern furniture and art with furnishings from all over the world. International eclecticism is new to Santa Fe design, but it cherishes the skilled craftsmanship that has long been important here. At the same time this trend opens Santa Fe design to international influences, it has helped to bring Santa Fe design to an international audience. Santa Fe eclecticism shows designers around the world how to integrate Southwestern elements into a Chicago bungalow, a San Francisco Victorian, or a London penthouse.

Right: Design by Bob Peters

ENTRADAS

ENTRYWAYS

At the entrance of many Anasazi and Pueblo homes, a visitor would have encountered a ladder. Rooms in pueblos were often entered through a square hole cut in the ceiling, which also served as an escape hole for smoke from the fire pit. Classic Anasazi ladders were simply notches carved in logs in a zigzag pattern. The rough-cut pine and strap-leather ladders that you see in Santa Fe today are used more for decoration than utility.

During the Spanish colonial period, lumber was scarce, so haciendas had very few doors. Since there was a constant threat of invasion, limiting the number of doors also increased security. Most colonists simply covered their thresholds with a sheep, cow, or buffalo pelt. Only wealthy aristocrats had wooden doors, but these were simple, hand-hewn, and massive. Elaborate paneled and carved doors were reserved for missions and churches.

American army architecture employed much wider proportions for doors and windows than had previously been used in New Mexico. The officers' quarters at Fort Union display fancy, embellished front doors, graced by transom and sidelight windows. The houses at the fort also have New Mexico's first vestibules and these large central hallways were often the scene of lively officers' parties.

The railroad brought in manufactured doors, and some territorial-style adobe homes still have Eastlake or Queen Anne doors complete with stained or etched glass windows. Hispanic carpenters in rural villages, such as Los Luceros, Truchas, Chacón, and Cordova, were inspired by these American doors to make their own variations of molded and paneled front doors and screen doors.

The railroad also made it possible for people in Santa Fe and other New Mexico towns to build Victorian mansions with elaborate entry halls. These vestibules often featured rich oak paneling, built-in hall benches, coat racks, and closets, and offered entry into the parlor through paneled glass doors. Victorian entry halls also had grand staircases, which ascended dramatically to the house's second floor.

Elements of both territorial and Victorian vestibules can be seen in many newer Santa Fe homes, but other contemporary houses feature elaborately carved wooden doors, skylights, tile or brick floors, changes in floor levels, and curved walls. Decorating these spaces appropriately requires the careful selection of a few objects that are just right for the space. These might include a Navajo rug, a large plant in a ceramic pot, or interesting furniture, such as a colonial bench or a priest's chair.

Right: The subtle grace of this Moorish entrance arch invites guests to a home filled with visual delights. Designer James Jereb skillfully blends North African architecture with such New Mexican elements as a beamed ceiling, a cow skull, and azulejos *(Mexican glazed tiles).*

Left: Designer James Jereb has managed artfully to warm and refine this entryway that might otherwise have been overwhelmed by its enormous solar skylights. A carved tree softens the double glass-panel front doors, and green plants abound.

Left: Repeating vigas and wall openings create a powerful progression in this Carter/Satzinger design. The scallop-vaulted ceiling adds to the dramatic repetition.

Left: A solarium provides a graceful transition from outdoors to indoors. Projecting vigas and a series of French doors set up a pleasing rhythm that takes the design of the house beyond its efficient use of modular elements.

Above: A Taos blue door is a visual surprise in this uncluttered entry that is finished with simple vigas and clean stucco plaster. Mexican tiles in a handsome interlocked pyramid design on the step risers and classic weavings complete the design.

Above: This entry evokes the romance of the Santa Fe Trail. Gracious double doors open onto a colorfully landscaped yard, but you almost expect to see an ox-drawn wagon rumble through the entrance. Brick pavers and a transom window are also a gesture to times past.

Left: *This powerful soaring vestibule recalls the Victorian entrance halls of the railroad era. Although the house was recently designed by Kells and Craig Architects, its beveled, chiseled surfaces; irregular forms; and exuberant manipulation of pine are a delightful reinterpretation of the Queen Anne aesthetic.*

Below: *This low stone wall demonstrates the way in which architect Bruce Davis interprets Santa Fe design through his own modern sensibilities. The wall suggests Chaco masonry, but it is perfectly harmonious with the refined contemporary attitude of the rest of the house.*

Above: *Like all the doors Bruce Davis designed for this Santa Fe home, the front door is precise, planar, and handsome in its proportions. The intersections of wall and wood, glass and wood, and wood with wood are carefully and cleanly articulated.*

Left: This entry hall juxtaposes traditional and contemporary touches. The Southwestern feeling of the Mexican clay-tile floor, louvered skylight, and built-in banco are offset by the hand-carved jackrabbit, the dramatic cactus, and the muted tones of the cushions and quilted textile collage.

Above: The dramatically understated curved space of this entrance hall by Cherry/See Architects is enhanced by its eclectic furnishings. Construction materials are set forth honestly, and the skylight and track lights illuminate the few well-chosen plants and furnishings so that they maintain equal weight to the architecture.

Above: Rustic lodge poles dominate the foyer of this country home by architects Holmes, Sabatini, and Eeds. A high, irregular gabled ceiling is enhanced by pine tongue-and-groove planking. The central staircase is flooded theatrically with sunlight, but the furnishings are folksy and keep the country mood relaxed.

Left: *This courtyard entrance offers a refreshing and innovative juxtaposition of traditional building elements. The flagstone patio is common in Santa Fe, but the masonry is random and organic.*

Right: *Four columns supporting a roof of lodge-pole vigas create an outdoor room without walls, which is enhanced by a long adobe* banco. *The corbels themselves are graphic abstractions, beautifully notched to hold the lintels. A* ristra, *Mexican pots, an old chair, and colorful tapestries add spice to this enchanted space.*

Above: *The design of this entryway may have been influenced by West and North African architecture, but it is also distinctly New Mexican. The simple archway framed by a white painted stucco border demonstrates the compatibility of Islamic adobe architecture and Santa Fe design.*

Left: *This walkway conveys a feeling of order and mystery at the same time. Irregularly cut flagstone slabs float on a bed of cocoa-colored gravel. The rustic gate conceals a magical world to which a sinuous plaster snake points the way.*

Left: *This plaster lizard startles you with its simplicity.*

Right: This hallway seems timeless thanks to the simple soft curve of the thick adobe archway intersected by brick steps. An unusual chair/table is the focal point of the landing. It contrasts richly with a Navajo rug and a Plains Indian war shield.

Far right: Pottery House was designed by Frank Lloyd Wright in 1942 and built in 1985. It is Wright's only adobe house. The weathered furniture and stylized ceiling vigas hint at Santa Fe style, but the expansive interlocking interior space of the circular hallway is pure Wright.

Left: Elegant and formal, this entrance hall is a study in symmetry. Strong rhythms are established by the ceiling vigas, the tiles embedded in the wall above the window, the bold diagonals on the door, and the rich pattern in the rug. Wiggly cactus shapes create visual tension, and a Moorish arch gives the illusion of a framed abstract design.

Above: This entrance is classically formal. The symmetrical arrangement of columns, corbels, ceramic urns, and ristras is not broken up by any clutter. The paneled door with its sidelights is locked into position by a low-lying dado strip.

73

SALAS

LIVING ROOMS

There is only one requirement for a Santa Fe *sala,* or living room: It must have a fireplace. This can be a traditional corner beehive fireplace, a territorial hearth positioned in the center of a wall with a plain or decorative mantel, or any contemporary variation on these themes. The style is not particularly important, but winter in Santa Fe without a cracking piñon fire is unimaginable.

During the Spanish colonial period, the *sala* was the room in which the family lived day and night. It contained the family's most valued possessions: a wooden chest, or *caja*; a few straight chairs; and perhaps a small table or priest's chair. A *repisa,* or wall shelf, with scalloped edges and scroll-cut end boards, may have held the family's *santos* and *retablos,* or these sacred objects may have been kept in a *nicho* cut into one of the room's adobe walls. Floors evolved from packed earth to wooden planks, brick, or baked ceramic tile, which made the *sala* warmer and easier to keep clean.

When the Americans arrived in Santa Fe, they transformed the *sala* into a formal sitting room. Between 1880 and 1920 living rooms in Santa Fe reflected the popular taste for Victorian furniture, textiles, and interior decor. After 1920 when the pueblo revival became the dominant trend in Santa Fe design, many New Mexican living rooms were redecorated with furniture and accessories that clearly showed their Pueblo and Spanish heritage.

Contemporary Santa Fe *salas* combine the best of the old with the new. Antique furniture, which can be New Mexican, Mexican, or Victorian, is often an important element of a room's design. Old Pueblo pottery and Hispanic religious art combine with Navajo rugs to create eclectic rooms with a sense of history. But antiques and special objects don't get in the way of comfort. The furniture people actually sit on and stretch out on must be comfortable above all else, so the sofas and chairs in a Santa Fe living room are likely to be modern and overstuffed with plenty of soft pillows. Fabrics often reflect the Southwestern landscape in their color and texture. Most designers prefer natural fibers and leather to synthetics. Flagstone, sometimes carved with petroglyphs, is often used for tabletops, and brightly painted and whimsical furniture contrasts pleasantly with antiques. Santa Fe design combines interesting objects, comfortable furniture, bold geometric patterns, and the soft organic colors of the room's architecture to create a warm, beautiful *sala* that welcomes home a family and their guests.

Right: A picture-perfect view of the Sandia Mountains, bright sunlight, and a pitched, gabled ceiling offset the huge corner beehive fireplace. An area rug that harmonizes with stencil designs on the wall and hearth brings the room together to make a unified statement about Santa Fe design at its best.

Right: *This delightful* sala *features a chip-carved Taos bed and matching coffee table. Navajo rugs warm the tile floor underneath the watchful gaze of a kachina doll on the mantel.*

Left: *Architects Carter/Satzinger delight in crafting unique pine-framed windows and doors. The lofty ceiling of this living room allows them to create a progression of large ground-floor patio doors as well as a small clerestory window with a deep reveal that emphasizes the great mass of the wall.*

Left: *Terraced half walls join lovely corbeled columns and a high clerestory window to produce a handsome dividing wall, which artfully separates the dining room from the living room. A painting by Fritz Scholder, a stunning turquoise* trastero, *and a unique* latilla *branch coffee table echo the high quality of the room's architectural details.*

Right: *From the geometric viga ceiling resting on great pine lintels to the classic profile of the fireplace and the Mexican tiles paving the floor, this room is a Southwestern masterpiece.*

Left: The high, gabled ceiling and rhythmic geometry of the door screens and dining room window make this room by Robert Strell a classic. Subtle touches, such as the paired ceramic urns and the ceiling molding, reinforce the formal organization of the room, while the use of latillas, adobe, *and willow-twig screens makes the* sala *an enchanting blend of classic Santa Fe design themes.*

Left: The unusual Art Deco lines of this adobe fireplace are offset by the gilded mirror and bas-relief as well as the summer flowers arranged in a basket in the hearth. Even without a blazing fire the large, plump throw pillows, comfortable chair, and cozy sofa make this room warm and inviting.

Right: Charles-David Interiors created this room with a view. Contemporary Santa Fe furnishings join colonial and Pueblo artifacts in a cozy setting that encourages conversation.

Left: A molded plywood-and-leather lounge chair and ottoman, designed by Charles Eames in 1956, look right at home beside a subtly curving banco *in this Taos living room. You might describe the style as organic minimalism.*

Left: The stripes of light produced by the ceiling skylights create an expansive progression of space that invites movement within. In this setting the central banco *becomes a powerful focus both architecturally and psychologically.*

Left: The built-in bancos *beneath walls of square windows are a modern, above-ground equivalent of the perimeter seating in a Pueblo kiva. This profusion of windows makes the Santa Fe foothills an integral part of the interior rather than just a panoramic view.*

Above: *Albuquerque architect Van Gilbert has made this room a masterful exercise in interlocking, intersecting spatial and visual forces. A diagonal stairway pierces the otherwise rigid grid composed of walls, glass planes, and voids. The strict geometry is also broken up by the elaborate, formal furnishings, which are carefully placed throughout the room.*

Above: *Tesuque sunlight floods this living room through a clerestory grid. This baroque lighting device illuminates many colonial mission churches in New Mexico, and recently clerestories have become a design element favored by solar architects.*

Left: Amy Walton's skillful and subtle design seems to turn its back on the room's traditional Santa Fe design elements of mellow maize-colored walls and a corner fireplace. But the English antiques in this room are kept from being overly conservative by bright rugs and other decorative objects that definitely give the room a sunny disposition.

Right: Hearth and gable mean comfort and security to many people, and in this room they are the dominant design features. The facade of the fireplace is elegant, precise, and classic in its formal symmetry and proportions. While the mass and color of the walls hint at the Southwest, this magnificent fireplace is an expression of a purely American design theme.

Above: A central tin lighting fixture and handsome plank-and-beam ceiling give this living room a New Mexico touch. Architects Kells and Craig have blessed their room with abundant windows and sunlight, and the panoramic view is the composition's most important decorative feature.

83

Right: The log walls, gabled roof beams, and cross braces establish a pattern of repeating triangles in this sophisticated log house. The central diamond gable window and pine-and-willow armoire pick up the triangular theme, but the rectangular glass doors establish a strong human zone that's echoed in the room's furnishings.

Right: In this dynamic living area, symmetry and order give way to slashing diagonals and irregularity. A ladder invites climbers to a gabled loft, filled with bright sunlight. The furnishings and the rich use of wood give the house an easy comfort.

Left: This updated ranch house by architects Johnson, Nestor, Mortier, and Rodriguez remembers New Mexico's long tradition of log architecture; the Spanish built stables and storage buildings of notched logs as did American homesteaders. The rustic stone fireplace, which has cousins in many cabins in the high forests, is the room's central design element.

Right: When Americans began building with adobe in about 1850, they made wooden mantels for their fireplaces, like the one in this living room. Despite its strong historic roots, the room's furniture encourages lounging—eating a taco on the small country table, reading in the ladder-back rocking chair, or snoozing on the sofa. A primitive antique Mexican colonial coffee table sits on an ornate, exuberant Oriental rug—an intriguing study of contrast.

Left: *This sunken living room in Santa Fe has an unpretentious, comfortable style. The pigskin-and-cedar Mexican* equipale *chair would be a good place to enjoy a book and a mug of hot chocolate. But even though the room is casual, every detail has been given careful attention. The half-wall opening is handsomely sculpted, and the room is accented with woven pillows from nearby Chimayo, Pueblo pots, and Apache baskets.*

Right: *This* sala *is entered through a wide adobe archway, in which each imperfect adobe brick is defined. A pair of double serrated diamond designs in the Navajo chief's blanket seems to point the way into the sitting area that is warmed by an adobe hearth. From the brick floors to the* latilla *ceiling, this room is an outstanding example of Santa Fe design.*

Above: *Elk antlers, potted cactus, and a fine painting of an Indian warrior let you know this* sala *by Kailer-Grant Designs is in New Mexico. A colonial table employed as a sofa table, contemporary wrought-iron candlesticks, and a case of kachina dolls complete the scene.*

87

Left: With its sinuous chimney flue, this massive beehive fireplace might have been the focal point of the room, but it is no match for the view of hills blanketed with junipers and piñons. The ceiling with its cedar *latilla* planking and traditional corbels is also stunning, but again the large picture windows hold our attention.

Below: This *sala* in the home of painter Fremont Ellis has been restored to the way it looked during the 1920s and 1930s. The room is a careful blend of Spanish colonial and Victorian furniture with traditional adobe architecture.

Above: Italian leather sofas effortlessly adapt to life in this mountain retreat in Placitas. Their sophisticated comfort fits in beautifully with the room's Southwestern design elements—walls given surface decoration by emphasizing the mortar joints around each adobe brick, an Apache basket on the mantel, and a Navajo Two Gray Hills tapestry.

Above: Lush plants and rattan furniture turn this room into a tropical oasis without eclipsing its Southwestern style. An international collection of furnishings works well with the tile floor, adobe fireplace, and generous arched windows.

89

Left: *In this Santa Fe living room, Westwork Architects created a contemporary scene with minimalist precision. The clean lines of the room are a counterpoint to kachina dolls, Navajo rugs, Pueblo pottery, and a Taos drum. The* sala *is also given a hearty share of Southwestern warmth by a deep-relief sunburst that crowns the fireplace, a Taos bed, and handsome planking.*

Left: *This hearth has a primeval presence that recalls both a prehistoric fire pit and also a Spanish shepherd's fireplace, which had a low shelf above the fire that was used as a food warmer as well as a cozy perch on which to sleep. This great piece of adobe sculpture is enhanced with a classic Apache basket decorated with ancient swastika symbols, a neatly stacked pile of firewood, and many fine Pueblo pots.*

Above: *Sandblasted wood, tropical plants, and adobe architecture produce a lush environment that welcomes quiet conversation. Family and guests sit comfortably on a generous freestanding* banco *that is the room's main piece of furniture.*

91

Left: This room has it all: dramatic architecture, fine paintings, comfortable and distinguished furniture, and a fascinating collection of crafts. The lighting is a dazzling combination of the sublime, the dramatic, and the primal. The night sky becomes deepening shades of Prussian blue as the fire roars below. Hidden spotlights beneath the lintel showcase a Fritz Scholder painting on the mantel that is flanked by Acoma pots. Randy Lee White's painting of a warrior and buffalo is displayed on another wall, and leather side chairs introduce a dash of European modernism in contrast with the antique colonial sofa table.

Above right: Very thick adobe walls allow for the carving out of lovely niches and windows. Adobe also terraces the mantel so that it becomes a stage on which to display treasured objects. Navajo rugs add dramatic color to a room that might seem subdued without them.

Right: The drama in this room is created by two viga columns. One is a simple post and lintel; the other boasts a corbel. The columns are echoed by the rounded vigas of the ceiling, which make such an important design statement that the architect has wisely chosen to place the windows relatively low in the walls.

Left: Descending into this living room, guests are welcomed by the corner fireplace in the winter or French doors in fair weather, when the adjoining patio provides the sala *with a delightful fresh-air annex.*

Right: This is Santa Fe design in the grand tradition. The dramatic spatial extensions of the room are further emphasized by the window placement and fenestration, while huge rustic tree-trunk columns define a cozier room within a room. Hidden lighting at split-level outlines traditional pots and a Navajo rug.

Left: This exquisite and highly original sala has at least two focal points: a carved stone fireplace mantel in a Mexican colonial spirit and a highly carved, spiraling column that rests on an adobe banco. Below the column, a kachina doll and hide tom-tom are displayed on a unique table composed of a slab of sandstone and glass.

Above: Interlocking ceiling beams create a stunning web of pine, establishing the structural and spatial matrix of the room. Concentric ovals sculpt the walls and the ceiling, which terraces back to a central soaring vortex. The geometric pattern of the floor tile repeats the pattern established in the ceiling.

Left and below: Architects McHugh, Lloyd, and Associates of Santa Fe planted twin corbeled columns in the entrance to this living room. Terraced half walls zigzag away, becoming wonderful pedestals for masterful Pueblo pottery, such as the Acoma bird olla. An antique colonial bench and table, ladder-back arm chairs, carved colonial retablo, kachina doll, and baskets fill out this delightful room.

Above: In the old way, adobe walls were hand-plastered with fine mud and straw paste by women called enjarradoras. The same skill and care with which these master plasterers worked give this room a quality of warmth and comfort. The tin-framed mirror, kerosene lamp, small crucifix, and the painting of Pueblo Buffalo dancers as well as the pitcher of mountain wildflowers on the table were carefully chosen to give the room a strong sense of nostalgia and romance. But the Taos bed was placed near the fireplace strictly for comfort.

Left: Architects Holmes, Sabatini, and Eeds demonstrate the universal adaptability of the Southwestern architectural style. Here vigas are stripped of corbels to become a streamlined structural skeleton, but they still retain their inherent Southwestern personality. Window grids are softened with curtains, but even traditional furnishings can't quell this room's strong sense of the new.

97

COMEDORES

DINING ROOMS

The informal warmth of Santa Fe dining rooms reflects a New Mexican tradition steeped in centuries of history. Above all the *comedor* is characterized by a love of Santa Fe's distinctive cuisine and the time-honored ways of serving and eating it. New Mexico's basic foods have always been eaten by hand. As most Americans know, tortillas take the place of both silverware and dishes when you eat tacos, nachos, burritos, or enchiladas.

The Anasazi people did not have dining rooms in their pueblos, and they never used any kind of eating utensils, plates, or tables. They ate tortillas, which had been developed by earlier cultures in Mexico, and since the time of the Anasazi, corn tortillas have been the heart of the Southwestern diet. The early people filled their tortilla "plates" with beans, chiles, and meat, and from these simple ingredients, a panoply of delightful and delicious foods has developed.

By the time Spanish colonists settled in New Mexico, Europeans had been living in Mexico for nearly one hundred years and were long familiar with New World foods and their preparation. The Spanish adopted Indian practices and enhanced them with their own culinary contributions, including beef, mutton, garlic, and rice. They also brought silverware, plates, glasses, cooking utensils, and the European custom of sit-down dining. But separate dining rooms were unknown in colonial New Mexico. Meals were eaten in the *sala*, which was also used for working, sleeping, entertaining, and most other family activities.

Many Americans who followed the Santa Fe Trail west expressed shock and disgust over the primitive, unsanitary eating habits of the New Mexicans. But many of them were also fascinated by the spicy and delectable foods.

The U.S. Army introduced separate dining rooms to New Mexico, and by the turn of the twentieth century, dining rooms were common here. The Victorian dining room may have prevailed architecturally, but the Indian and Spanish cuisine still predominates Santa Fe dining tables.

A meal served in Santa Fe is almost always a relaxed and sensual delight. Contemporary Santa Fe designers are fully aware of this when they construct dining rooms. Careful attention is given to light and its modulations, from glorious desert sunlight flooding in through a picture window to delicate beams of candlelight emanating from tin or wrought iron candelabra. Ceiling vigas, dramatic displays of wood, and a corner fireplace combine to create a romantic ambience in a traditional Santa Fe dining room. But anyone who is familiar with Santa Fe knows that the ambience of the room is less important than the food served there. A small neighborhood cafe or the *comedor* of your neighbor's *abuelita* (grandmother) is likely to be the best eating place of all.

Right: The mood of this dining room is romantic and mysterious. Guests are greeted by an arched entrance with a painted border and flanking teardrop wall sconces. The dark, brooding personality of the room is softened by its handcrafted furnishings. The ceiling vigas and earthen walls speak of Santa Fe, but they could also whisper "Marrakesh."

Left: *Soft New Mexico pastels color this sophisticated dining room. The table base and corner screen made of* latillas *add a distinctly Southwestern accent to the otherwise eclectic international decor of the room. Plants, the painting, and a folk-carved pig punctuate the scene with whimsy.*

Right: *This simple but dramatic room is enhanced by its beautiful wall openings—double glass doors leading to the backyard and a terraced adobe half wall framing the kitchen. The rattan dining chairs and* latilla *table base harmonize with the Oriental carpet and natural finishes of the room. The tangled wrought-iron chandelier is the room's focal point.*

Above: *Many of the classic elements of Santa Fe design blend together effortlessly in this room. An antique rough-hewn dining table is set off by worn, painted side chairs. A century-old* trastero *boasts a Yankee influence in the star pattern on its punched-tin panels. The lithograph is a tribute to Zuni Pueblo artifacts. Candlelight bathes the earth-plastered walls with a sensuous glow.*

Right: Bauhaus design is given a Southwestern accent in this dining room. The polished stone floor and sleek leather-and-chrome dining furniture speak of cool European design sophistication. They contrast and blend with the rustic ceiling vigas and antique sideboard in an inspired mix.

Above: This room needs only a few subtle references to achieve a sophisticated Santa Fe style. In addition to the view, there are paneled double doors.

Below: In Frank Lloyd Wright's Pottery House built in Santa Fe in 1985, the Mexican colonial dining table and chairs provide a baroque counterpoint to the otherwise austere character of the room.

Left: *This room has a seductive, sculptural feel that is established by the graceful rhythm of its arched openings, the shallow barrel-vaulted ceiling, its generous niches, organic capitals, and massive double-hearth fireplace. The room's personality is autumnal; it is the perfect setting for a glorious Thanksgiving or Christmas dinner.*

Right: *The dining room in this house seems to be almost crushed by the tremendous force of the pitched pine ceiling. But a generous amount of New Mexican sunlight pouring in through triple glass patio doors keeps this modest* comedor *from becoming oppressive. The space radiates homey comfort, which is a hallmark of understated Santa Fe design.*

Above: *Pine timbers shoulder a marvelous series of barrel-vaulted ceilings, each with a different curvature and length. The table is located at an intersection of spatial and visual forces, including hallways that branch off and a glorious view. The furnishings are a mix of contemporary, classical, and Southwestern.*

Left: Mexican-tile steps beckon guests upward to an elegant dining room in this house designed by Bob Peters. The length of the room is enhanced by a built-in banco on one side of the modern oval dining table. The walls are delicately tapered and finished with egg-shell precision, and the herringbone pattern of the latilla-and-viga ceiling is an exercise in traditional craftsmanship.

Above right: This dining room and entertainment alcove pushes Santa Fe design to classic formalism. Symmetry and rhythm give the room a calm order. The inherent weight and mass of adobe architecture is set free by floating the ceiling on great timbers and columns.

Right: A central conservatory is the heart of this floor plan. It recalls the plazuela of Spanish colonial haciendas, but in this house traditional Southwestern design elements, such as vigas and corbels, join wooden screens and contemporary furnishings in a masterful and unexpected way.

Left: This house is a fascinating blend of primitive and contemporary elements. The division between interior and exterior space is blurred and ambiguous. In the dining room a monumental sculptured fireplace is a dramatic centerpiece among huge boulder walls, and the baroque side chairs and table add a civilized touch to the room.

COCINAS

KITCHENS

Santa Fe kitchens have a unique look and smell that is a direct result of the wonderful food produced there. Southwestern food is aromatic, colorful, exotic, invigorating, and delicious. When the Pueblo staples of corn, beans, squash, and chiles are prepared in a way that joins Spanish, Mexican, and Anglo cooking styles, the result is one of the world's most delectable regional cuisines.

New Mexico foodstuffs are often used to decorate and enliven Santa Fe *cocinas*. Garlic, zucchini, yellow squash, pumpkins, and multicolored Indian maize, look great in woven baskets or simply lying on a kitchen countertop made of colorful Mexican glazed tile. *Ristras* of red chiles hang in many kitchens.

Until about 1850 separate kitchens were a novelty in New Mexico, and it wasn't until cast-iron cookstoves could be brought in on the railroad that most Santa Fe homes began to devote an entire room to cooking. But the advantages of cooking on a stove as opposed to struggling with an open hearth quickly made a cookstove an essential part of every home. In some mountain villages, houses had cookstoves many decades before they got indoor plumbing and electricity. Today antique black-and-chrome cookstoves are often the pride of Santa Fe kitchens. But some cooks and decorators prefer the colored porcelain-enamel stoves that were first produced during the 1920s. It is not unusual for a Santa Fe kitchen to have either one of these styles of old stoves as well as a modern cooktop and built-in oven.

Cabinets in a Santa Fe kitchen are likely to be handcrafted of pine or cedar. Many are embellished with Southwestern design motifs such as sun symbols, crosses, zigzags, or hearts. A *trastero,* or cupboard, augments the contemporary cabinets in many kitchens. Some *trasteros* are handpainted, and others have punched tin doors similar to pie safes found in other parts of the country. Rustic wooden chopping blocks sit in the middle of many Santa Fe *cocinas,* and Mexican ceramic tiles are used on countertops and floors. These tiles are easy to clean and complement other natural surfaces in the kitchen.

Right: This Santa Fe kitchen may look rustic, but it is thoroughly modern in its conveniences. The multicolored brick, hand-scraped vigas, hanging Apache baskets, Indian maize, and drying herbs are organic and earthy, while the modular cooktop, double ovens, and microwave offer state-of-the-art cooking efficiency.

Left: *This small* cocina *by Cherry/ See Architects is expanded visually by the wonderful fireplace and the terrific view of the mountains. The space is also made to seem larger by the cleanly designed appliances that blend in well with the brick floor and wooden cabinets.*

Above right: *Glazed Mexican tiles add lively color to the wood surface of the cabinets and the natural finishes of the vigas and brick floor.*

Right: *This kitchen area is defined by an unplastered adobe brick wall and pilaster, which provide support for the great ceiling vigas. The rough adobe and the vigas contrast nicely with the smooth, sculptural plastered walls and the kitchen's custom pine cabinets.*

Left: *Adorned by* ristras *of garlic and chiles, a notched-beam cooking pavilion holds center stage in this northern New Mexico farmhouse. Along with the antique furniture, which includes a spindle* trastero, *weathered blue side chairs with woven seats, and a primitive bench, the row of antique cooking pottery atop the cabinets makes a charming scene.*

Left: *A gorgeous adobe wall ennobled by formal, symmetrical windows complements the European design of this kitchen's cabinets and fixtures. Terrific attention to detail, such as the glass block of the sink counter, the louvered door, and antique dining table, compound the visual interest of this striking blend of traditional and modern Santa Fe design.*

Right: *Placed in a pure-white design scheme, Eurostyle cabinets work well with glazed Mexican tiles. The hand-carved pine column with interlocking corbel and broad lintels becomes the central axis around which this entire composition revolves. But without the unusually high ceilings, the room might lose its airy, refreshing quality.*

Below: *In this special kitchen design, architect Bob Peters combines the most advanced cooking equipment with abstracted, modernist Southwestern details. Gleaming white Eurostyle cabinets contrast strongly with the violet window wall. Without ornamentation, the ceiling beams float above the interior. Peters deliberately kept the windows small and cubical, so they yield only teasing peeks of the piñon-clad hills outside.*

Right: *Light, air, and clean lines make this kitchen a welcome addition to the great room of a remodeled Santa Fe home. A boomerang half wall hides kitchen mess and acts as a comfortable place to eat breakfast or visit the cook without getting in his or her way.*

Left: *Small glazed tiles create bold patterns of concentric spiral swirls on the countertops and wall. These patterns are echoed in the oval roof shelf and cabinet bracket mounts.*

Left: *Despite a few modern updates, this kitchen remains a 1940s classic. The central attraction is the enameled gas stove with its charming hood. The painted paneled door is derived from turn-of-the-century folk-carpentry doors, and the Mexican tiles and a carved mirror create the mood of a Hispanic cocina.*

Above: *Frank Lloyd Wright rarely designed architecturally significant kitchens for his houses, but in the kitchen of Pottery House, the view of the Sangre de Cristo Mountains more than makes up for the room's small dimensions. The superb cabinetwork creates a beautiful frame for the wondrous scenery outside.*

Right: Studio Arquitectura builds in Spanish ambience with dark stained pine beams and woodwork, brick, and adobe. Custom cabinets with spindle doors, an unusual wrought-iron chandelier, and an antique dining table reinforce this Old World theme.

Below: A Mexican glazed-tile oven hood is the centerpiece of this kitchen. But a bouquet of dried maize, polished copper kettles, a chile ristra *hung outside the window, a woven bread basket, and a pot of forced bulbs add homey, lived-in comfort.*

Right: Restaurant cooking equipment vies with exotic detailing in this large cocina *by Studio Arquitectura. Folk-painted columns, a pressed-tin ceiling, a Moorish wall shelf, a blue window frame, adobe walls, and a tile floor combine to give the kitchen a romantic flavor. But a serious cook will also appreciate expansive countertops, excellent lighting, and easy access to his or her pots and pans.*

Right: *This turn-of-the-century Victorian house in Silver City, a mining town in southwestern New Mexico, boasts a fine traditional kitchen. The restoration shows a keen appreciation of such American standards as the round oak dining table, butcher's block, antique cast-iron cookstove, and bentwood high chair.*

Left: *In this straight-forward Santa Fe kitchen, glazed tile interprets geometric motifs in desert colors. The terraced design of the tiles neatly follows the contours of cabinets and terraced wall opening, adding a touch of color without disrupting the kitchen's clean lines.*

Below: *Detailing on the custom wooden cabinets gives this kitchen a colonial feeling, but the expansive space and modern cooking equipment encourage efficient food preparation and a smooth traffic flow. Like the kitchen as a whole, the hanging wrought-iron kitchen caddy filled with gleaming copper utensils and suspended from the lofty ceiling is both beautiful and efficient.*

Right: *French doors with glass knobs open into this Santa Fe kitchen that is a pleasant blend of design styles. The rich pattern of flagstone and Mexican tiles in the floor and the double, shallow ceiling vaults that terminate in vigas are examples of Santa Fe style at its best, while the large panels of copper warm the room with a special glow.*

Left: *These distinctive kitchen cabinets are stained Taos blue—an unusual color for the kitchen. But Kailer-Grant Designs uses this strong turquoise as a contrast to the terra-cotta glazed tiles and salmon-colored walls, which are modern construction that has been made to resemble adobe. The playful demons on bicycles are painted ceramic sculptures from the central Mexican state of Morelia.*

Right: *Tiles, cabinets, and kitchen equipment form a simple but effective geometric harmony in this Taos kitchen, which is complemented by the pine plank floor and dark-toned vigas.*

Above: *These kitchen cabinets provide a strong design statement; they are streamlined but still retain a natural wood finish. The revealed lintel above rounded threshold columns contrasts pleasingly with the cabinets, as does the wall color, the art, and the small, recessed window over the sink.*

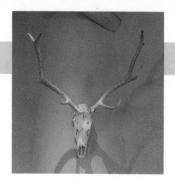

LUGARES de RETIRO

DENS

In a pueblo or a colonial hacienda, one room had to be adapted to meet all a family's needs for interior space. Specialized rooms, such as dens, home offices, studies, studios, and libraries, were unknown in New Mexico until very recently, and many New Mexicans still use the same table for dining, playing cards, and doing the books. The archaeologists and artists who came to Santa Fe during the first part of the twentieth century were probably the first people to establish offices and studios in their adobe homes. But the idea of setting aside rooms for single purposes has been slow to catch on, since only a few people boast large collections of books or other precious objects and require a place to store and display them.

The advent of telecommunicating and the recent explosion of reading material (evidenced by the launching of 2,500 new magazines during the 1980s) have made having a quiet place to read and work at home less of a luxury and more of a necessity for many people. If you have a telephone line, a home computer, a copying machine, and a fax machine, your home, even if it's deep in the mountains, can be an ideal place to work. Especially in relatively isolated places like Santa Fe, more and more people are working at home and doing the same kind of work they used to do in of-

fices. People are also moving to Santa Fe to escape the frantic pace of larger urban areas because they are able essentially to bring their jobs with them.

While some dens and libraries in Santa Fe homes are making way for home office equipment, others are adding more comfortable chairs, better reading lamps, and a cozy wood stove. These are true *lugares de retiro,* places to get away from it all and relax with a good book. Collections of fine pottery and favorite books sit comfortably on shelves. They are displayed not only to be admired but also to be studied and appreciated. Like all rooms of Santa Fe design, dens are comfortable and welcoming.

Whether a Santa Fe study is set up as a home office that is electronically connected to the outside world or as a quiet retreat from that world, it is tempered with the intangible charms of New Mexico: clear, beautiful light; clean, invigorating air; and a scenery that tends to rearrange priorities. Many people in Santa Fe have learned to put spirit, culture, and intellect ahead of purely commercial pursuits. Contemporary Santa Fe dens and home offices reflect this relaxed work ethic. Easy chairs, the nearby fireplace, and Southwestern cultural treasures are the most appropriate studio furnishings.

Right: A worldly bazaar of cultural artifacts and antiques gives every corner of this studio designed by James Jereb a lively presence. North African tapestries resonate powerfully against the rust, indigo, and umber walls. The painted ceiling and floor-tile pattern bridge Southwestern and Islamic traditions, and the familiar corner fireplace is enhanced by the application of color, stenciled symbols, and terraced half walls.

Above: *The glazed-tile fountain and high, paneled shutters give this lounge by Studio Arquitectura a decidedly Spanish character. The richness of the room is developed further by the lovely cardinal-red rattan chairs that harmonize beautifully with the Oriental rug and intense-green plants.*

Above: *The strong lines of this backlighted bookcase contrast with the rounded elements of a beautiful display of Pueblo pottery. The polychrome Acoma olla on top of the case, the classic black San Ildefonso pottery on the top shelf, and the historic Hopi pots below are the highlights of this fine collection.*

Above: *In his design for Pottery House, Frank Lloyd Wright adapted Southwestern architectural conventions in his own inimitable way. Here he abstracted the corner fireplace into a huge bell and streamlined the adobe banco to conform to the proportions of the windows and bubble clerestory rows.*

Left: *The ceiling of this magnificent study is a tic-tac-toe of vigas, dotted by sunken spotlights. Willow-twig shutters dim the afternoon light or open wide to reveal glorious desert vistas. The room's sense of territorial style is fully developed in the dentil motif that runs around the top of the built-in bookcases.*

Right: *The symmetrical placement of pictures, plants, and furniture gives this room a formal order, which is echoed by the tidy arrangement of Pueblo pots, books, and other family favorites on the wall shelves. But the bold Navajo rug from Ganado, Arizona, is a strong design element that expands on this carefully constructed symmetry.*

Left: *Westwork Architects chose to place a cast-iron wood stove in an unusual setting in this study. But it harmonizes beautifully with the cut-out deco wall insert; streamlined, wrap-around windows; Eames chair; and the post-modern design attitude of the desk.*

Far left: *Because a traditional Spanish fireplace pulls people away from the center of the room, the designer of this den chose to focus attention on the corner by adding an undulating, layered decorative wall.*

Above: *In this cozy sitting area, the half wall is projected spatially upward by the viga and corbel above it, creating a dramatic setting for an unusually round, onion-shaped corner fireplace, which has a surprisingly Oriental profile.*

Left: *This large cast-iron wood stove keeps this office cozy all winter, while the windows, French doors, and clerestory warm the room with bright sunlight. A collection of Mexican masks and stained glass windows provides additional charm in this lively room.*

Below: *This graceful arched entrance, which is unusual in Santa Fe design, seems to flutter in space by virtue of a strong scalloped border design. It coaxes a guest to come in and sit down by a fire in the half-barrel hearth, but the arch also conceals the mystery of a studio filled with African treasures.*

Above: *Architect Bruce Davis and solar builder Karen Terry collaborated on this house. The result is a cheerful interior filled with generous daylight and expansive, interlocking spaces.*

ALCOBAS

BEDROOMS

The Spanish colonists did little to advance the cause of comfortable sleeping in New Mexico. They slept on sheepskin pelts laid on earthen *bancos* or directly on the floor, much as the Pueblos had done for a thousand years. The idea of setting aside a room especially for sleeping was unheard of in New Mexico until the opening of the Santa Fe Trail. But regular trade with Missouri and the presence of the army quickly changed this. By the middle of the nineteenth century, Empire-style bed frames and daybeds were regularly imported into New Mexico, and native carpenters had begun to imitate them, coming up with their own distinctive variations. By the turn of the century, bedrooms were as common in Santa Fe as they were in other parts of the country, and most Santa Fe *alcobas,* with their steel or cast-iron bed frames, looked like bedrooms any place else in the U.S. Bedroom furniture and accessories that are distinctively Santa Fe design have only recently been introduced.

Closets and chests of drawers were also unheard of in New Mexico until the arrival of the Americans. The Spanish colonists had kept the few fancy clothes they owned in *cajas,* or wooden chests. But American furniture styles were quickly adopted. Today armoires, which were common in New Mexico during the territorial period, are back in vogue in Santa Fe as they are in other parts of the country. An armoire may be used to store clothes, but it is equally likely to be an entertainment center. In some New Mexican *alcobas, trasteros* are used as armoires; other modern adobe bedrooms are given an eclectic touch by the addition of a Victorian or Mexican dresser.

In Santa Fe four-poster beds, which are enjoying a resurgence of popularity everywhere, are often made of massive lodge poles that have been stripped of bark and varnished or oiled. Matching bedside tables, chairs, and other bedroom furniture are also made in this rustic lodge-pole style. Other Santa Fe bedrooms combine a lodge-pole bed with bedside tables that are hand-painted folk-art pieces or colonial antiques. Lamps with Pueblo or Mexican pottery bases and shades made of copper or tin with delicate punched hole patterns provide soft bedside lighting. These special lamps may be difficult to find outside of Santa Fe, but finding the appropriate bed linen for a Santa Fe *alcoba* is certainly no problem, since many designers have created collections that have Southwestern design themes and soft desert colors.

Right: Warm adobe walls become a backdrop for a meeting of commercial structural elements and traditional Santa Fe furnishings in this house by designer Robert Strell. The cathedral ceiling of the bedroom is articulated by rhythmic gable rafters with pendulum industrial light fixtures peeking in between. Victorian furniture and accents mix easily with a Southwestern night lamp and plaque baskets.

Left: Hardwood and adobe give this Tesuque bedroom a stately, dignified feeling. Much of this spirit emanates from the solid Italianate bed frame. But the pastels of the bed's quilt add a dash of color.

Left: Designer Clorinda Shook has recreated a traditional American bedroom in this territorial-style home. Opposing windows cut out of a steep gable give the room an angular, airy character. Double glass doors open onto a balcony, where a glorious desert view is sure to enhance a leisurely cup of morning coffee and the Sunday paper.

Above: Violet is an unusual color for a Santa Fe interior. But in this bedroom lavender, fuchsia, and indigo harmonize well with the Tiffany glass night lamps and an assortment of Pueblo pots perched on the terraced half wall. A solitary kachina doll keeps watch on the horno (fireplace).

133

■ **Right:** *This bedroom in a house designed by architects Holmes, Sabatini, and Eeds is reminiscent of a Victorian-adobe parlor. The* latilla *herringbone ceiling and cut-out wall sequence are a wonderful architectural progression, dividing the room into zones for sleeping, sitting, and entertaining. The colonial-style* trastero *conceals a television set and other audio/video equipment.*

■ **Left:** *A solitary corbeled column commands the master bedroom of this residence designed by Bob Peters. The architectural canopy creates a hierarchy of space within the towering vertical dimensions of the room. The furnishings are well-known elements of Santa Fe design: pigskin and cedar* equipale *furniture from Mexico, a modern lodge-pole pine study table, and a rug with a Saltillo diamond design.*

■ **Above:** *The warmth of pine creates a cozy feeling in this small bedroom, but ample windows bring in spectacular views of the vast New Mexican horizon. The cast-iron Victorian bed frame is a lacy delight that contrasts elegantly with the straight lines of the room's architecture.*

■ **Above:** *Lovely clerestory light washes down an entire wall of this bedroom by Santa Fe architects Johnson, Nestor, Mortier, and Rodriguez. Double, carved-panel doors offer access to the room through a deep adobe wall. The elegant iron four-poster bed is a contemporary classic that reflects a post-modern fascination with traditional furniture prototypes.*

Left: Real adobe walls are the unmistakable trademark of the superb craftsmanship of this Santa Fe home. In keeping with the historic and unpretentious character of the room, an antique wooden chest sits in its traditional place at the foot of the wooden spindle bed.

Right: This bedroom shows a refined appreciation for folk art and furniture. Textiles provide the room's design motifs, while patterned quilts and the perched songbirds on the curtains play a supporting role to the lovingly carved coyote who wins our hearts.

Above: Adobe walls and pine plank floors give a lustrous natural glow to this bedroom. The furnishings are spare and true: Twin spindle-post bed frames painted French blue and an Oriental carpet are enough to satisfy.

137

Left: Patrician Design of Albuquerque used a careful mix of design themes to create this sumptuous bedroom. A heavy, dark Victorian armoire adds a bass note to an otherwise light and neutral color scheme, with carefully arranged pottery and a rustic lodge-pole bed frame lightened by a billowing comforter.

Above right: Ceiling vigas become exaggerated and powerful design elements in this bedroom. Vigas are usually connected with wood, either branch *latillas* or *planks*, but here plaster gives the wooden beams added intensity.

Right: This bedroom is sleek and modern, with a clever articulation of glass walls; soaring, volumetric spaces; and a cool palette of finishes, often pure white. Only the looming Sangre de Cristo Mountains give a hint that this house is in Tesuque.

Left: Bob Peters carefully combines the best Southwestern details of a viga ceiling, a corner *horno (fireplace),* and a low built-in banco *with a breathtaking picture window in this contemporary bedroom. No extraneous window frames or other moldings hinder the dazzling view that is echoed in the colors of the room.*

Right: *The Red Hills bed, shutters, and credenza in this room were made by Sombraje, a furniture studio in Dixon, New Mexico. In this lovely Hispanic village located in the mountains midway between Santa Fe and Taos, Sombraje pioneered the use of colorfully dyed willow twigs to create exquisite and classic furniture. The compelling personality of this bedroom is enhanced with the priest's chair by David Burke, pillows by Sara McCook, watercolors by Russel Hall, and a painting by Walter Green.*

Above left: *Contemporary Santa Fe design is the working aesthetic for this bedroom by Kailer-Grant Designs. Bold patterned bed covers establish the room's colors. The lamp tables and bed frames are inspired by the traditional craftsmanship of Spanish colonial furniture, and a lovely half-wall niche with opposing inset viga columns is a perfect place to display handsome pots and carvings.*

Left: *Niches create intimacy in a room, inviting people to exhibit their most prized and best loved objects. In this bedroom architect Bob Peters used niches of various sizes and placement to carve out more living space in a modest-sized room. The skylight also opens up the room, and the blue, gray, and brown colors combine to make a peaceful, meditative environment.*

Right: *Massive ceiling vigas placed close to each other create a striking rhythm. Built-in bookshelves and a true adobe threshold without a frame are fine details by architects Johnson, Nestor, Mortier, and Rodriguez.*

BAÑOS

BATHROOMS

Like many other modern conveniences, plumbing arrived fairly recently on the Southwestern frontier. Only a few Santa Fe homes had bathrooms before the late 1880s, and then only the extravagant Queen Anne and Italianate mansions. One truly astounding nineteenth century bathroom was built in the town of Las Vegas, New Mexico, by a wealthy lawyer named John Veeder. The bathroom is on the second floor of his opulent town house. In the middle of a room that's about the size of a modern living room, Veeder placed an oversized claw-foot bathtub. In one corner there's a head-to-toe shower made of a spiral of copper tubing pierced with tiny holes. The multidirectional shower drains into a marble slab on the floor. There is also a pedestal sink and many large mirrors. The walls are tiled to half height in ivory tiles, and a gold-leaf garland border completes the sumptuous scene. Paired stained-glass windows flood the room with pastel light. This palatial bathing facility was built at the same time most people in New Mexico were bathing in a basin and using an outdoor privy. It's just another example of the way in which the primitive and modern can exist simultaneously in New Mexico.

Many contemporary Santa Fe bathrooms aspire to the relaxed luxury of their Victorian predecessors, even when their designs suggest the rugged frontier or Spanish colonial simplicity. Bathrooms in Santa Fe, like those in other parts of the country, now occupy larger spaces than they used to, and designers often make this room the focus for a master suite rather than viewing the bathroom as a utilitarian afterthought. Tubs are becoming larger and deeper; they often defy standard builder's dimensions and require special installation. Many Santa Fe designers are playing with the infinite artistic potential of colored and glazed tiles. Ceramic tile is used not only on bathroom walls and floors but also to surface countertops, platforms for deep tubs, and window surrounds. Bathroom lighting is not restricted to electric light fixtures, but often incorporates skylights as well as colored or opaque glass. Hot tubs and whirlpool baths are common in the Southwest, and some homes have steam baths and saunas. A fashionable *baño* in Santa Fe has up-to-date technology beautifully executed with the light and colors of New Mexico.

Not everyone in New Mexico bathes only in the privacy of his or her own home. This area is blessed with many natural hot springs, and these magic pools of hot, healing mineral water are considered sacred and life restoring. Even in winter, people hike to remote hot springs to enjoy a picnic and soothing plunge. For the less adventurous, Santa Fe now boasts one Japanese bathhouse in the high-pine mountain country overlooking the city. In little over a century, bathing in New Mexico has made remarkable progress, but many Santa Fe natives vow that natural hot springs are the ultimate New Mexico splash.

Right: This tub alcove is classically formal and symmetrical, but it is softened by an ever-so-subtle modulation of color as shades of coral and turquoise flicker off the jazzy surfaces of handmade tiles, glass block, and adobe.

Left: *This tropical getaway is hardly a typical Santa Fe bath, but the tiles are handmade and the plasterwork is a variation on an old theme. The bas-relief is made of dyed plaster applied directly to the plaster wall.*

Right: *Prickly pear and barrel cactus, each in its own uniquely colored tile frame, form a playful zigzag of color that's a foil for the creamy, glossy surfaces of this bathroom.*

Above: *Santa Fe architect Bob Peters built this master bathroom around a central, tiled bathing pavilion. The tub itself becomes a dramatic space divider, enhanced by a skylight that crowns its regal stature.*

Below: *The washbasin and tub in this Victorian bathroom are timeless treasures, generous in proportion and lustre. Antique mirrors and pictures reflect an image of the past when good grooming was an art. A hand stenciled flower border rings the room.*

Above: *Handmade tiles expand even a standard-sized tub surround into a show of desert radiance. A ribbon of glass block breaks into this abstract melody of geometric expression.*

145

Right: Plaster animals and trees embossed on the wall give this otherwise sophisticated bathroom a Santa Fe touch of whimsy.

Left: The luxury of having an adobe corner fireplace in the bathroom is unsurpassed. A long soaking bath near a warm, flickering fire is the perfect antidote to a hard day. The sea shells embedded in the adobe are good-luck charms that are reminiscent of the bits of shell found in Anasazi ruins.

Above: At Mabel Dodge Luhan's house in Taos, painted glass effectively provides privacy for the bathroom. The classic pedestal sink hints at the room's age, but the glass painting that recalls the magic of a Taos afternoon is timeless.

Above: Towels stored in baskets and a sheep-skin rug bring a distinctly Santa Fe touch to this elegant bathroom.

PORTALES

PORCHES

Given New Mexico's spectacular natural setting, it is no wonder that *portales* and other outside living spaces, such as patios and gardens, are important elements of Santa Fe design. People here not only enjoy relaxed lounging in the semishelter of their porches at home, but more and more Santa Fe hotels and restaurants feature outdoor seating and dining. In summer along Canyon Road, many bistros serve food on *portales* and patios, sometimes accompanied by a flamenco guitar.

The oldest and most important *portal* in New Mexico is on the Palace of the Governors, the oldest public building in the United States. It was built in about 1610 on the Plaza in Santa Fe. The *portal* was altered in 1867 when territorial-style trim and scroll-sawn molding were added, but in 1909 the porch was restored to the way it looked during colonial times. This dramatic restoration inspired the Pueblo revival movement in architecture and design that is responsible for the way Santa Fe looks today.

Documented *portales* from the eighteenth century are rare; along with the governor's palace, there is a small balcony on the mission church in Acoma Pueblo. But by the end of the Spanish colonial period in the 1820s, wealthy landowners could afford covered porches and most added them to their haciendas. Many of these *portales* were placed on a southern or eastern exposure, usually at the intersection of two wings of the house.

The structure of *portales* consists of a horizontal timber placed parallel to the building's facade. This beam is supported by posts that are usually crowned with *zapatas* (corbels). The corbels transfer weight from the beam and porch roof onto the posts. Traditional *portal* roof construction is *viga* logs with branch *latillas* or planks between.

Since colonial days, *portales* have inspired countless architects, designers, and builders. The *zapata* itself, rooted in Hispanic and Islamic traditions, offers almost infinite design possibilities in profiling, chip carving, painting, applied ornament, and other variations. Once a porch is built, furnishing it is an enjoyable design task. To make a relaxed outdoor room, choose comfortable chairs and enough tables so that food, drinks, and reading material are within easy reach of every chair. Lush potted plants, cacti, an antique colonial bench, Pueblo artifacts, hanging *ristras,* herb wreaths, tin ornaments, and other favorite objects complete the scene. Just make sure that nothing blocks anyone's view of earth and sky.

Right: Smooth, built-up columns of Douglas fir pivot in series around this house. The architecture unites viga and post into one streamlined structural unit, supported at ground level by a wonderfully crafted planter wall of Chaco masonry.

Left: New Mexico has more than 300 sunny days throughout the year, so this large sun room is likely to be the most popular room in the house. The family uses the warm, bright space for dining, growing plants, and looking at the view.

Right: This spectacularly lit solarium is an enclosed variation on the colonial *portal.* The rhythm of the window framing is reminiscent of an orderly row of columns, while the extended vigas are a direct reference to New Mexican porches of the past.

Below: In this solarium precision-cut and fitted wooden beams create a tripartite window system of ceiling, picture window, and vent. The slightly projecting, angled roof glazing results in an unexpected eave.

Above: Architects Johnson, Nestor, Mortier, and Rodriguez designed this masterful contemporary *portal. Form and structure are pared down to essentials; only the Spanish fireplace and its terraced windbreak step outside the straightforward design.*

Left: Loosely covered over with slats, this portal offers only a little shade, but it casts a bold graphic pattern on the otherwise simple facade of this building.

Below: This gorgeous territorial-style veranda is the perfect place from which to watch a summer rainstorm. The columns are beautifully tapered, and the door and window pediments and shutters are well crafted in keeping with the period of the house.

Above: Large masonry pilasters support the structural and visual mass of adobe architecture. The flowing, organic quality of the portal is created by the pilasters, the curving house wall, the irregular-cut flagstone patio floor, and rough-cut pine ceiling beams.

Above: Under the simple portal of rough pine poles, a painted terraced border produces a powerful optical effect against a white background.

Above: Ken McKenzie was the architect for the extensive remodeling on this Santa Fe house that added a swimming pool set in a flagstone patio and a traditional portal, which shelters poolside guests from the intense sun.

Right: *This is truly an outdoor room that fuses porch and patio. The structure is an unorthodox application of vigas and adobe molded to a circular wall design. The unexpected is a trademark of this house, where even the contemporary patio furniture is a surprise.*

Left: *The veranda of painter Fremont Ellis's Santa Fe home is noble and classic, and complements the long facade of the artist's hacienda. The doors and windows boast elegant territorial moldings, and the windows are graced by shutters. The adzed columns are colonial antiques that lack corbels, but in this long* portal, *the rhythm and perspectives of the posts more than compensate for the missing corbels.*

Left: *The garden facade of this territorial-style house is organized around the central* portal. *This is consistent with its classic style; the symmetrical ordering of windows, walls, and columns; and their handsome proportions. The brickwork at roof level forms a lovely cornice.*

Above: *In this house the* portal *has been abstracted to its key elements, which are presented in earthen stucco. The angular forms of the passive-solar clerestory windows and projecting downspouts are also elemental, so that this design is as resonant as the Japanese bell in the garden.*

Left: This garden facade uses elements from Pueblo revival architecture, but they have been adapted in subtle ways to create a new design sensibility. Instead of a right angle intersection of house wings, the obtuse angle of this plan allows the portales *and parapets to create an interesting rhythm that is reinforced by the columns, corbels, vigas, and downspouts.*

Above: Solid, cleanly expressed geometry and earthen stucco combine in a design of sculptural primacy in this greenhouse. Heat storage cylinders and roll-down sunscreens, which help filter light and solar gain, improve the efficiency and enhance its design.

Above: The facade of this solar greenhouse with the stepped-up forms of its central pavilion is a formal composition, emphasizing symmetry and regular harmonies.

157

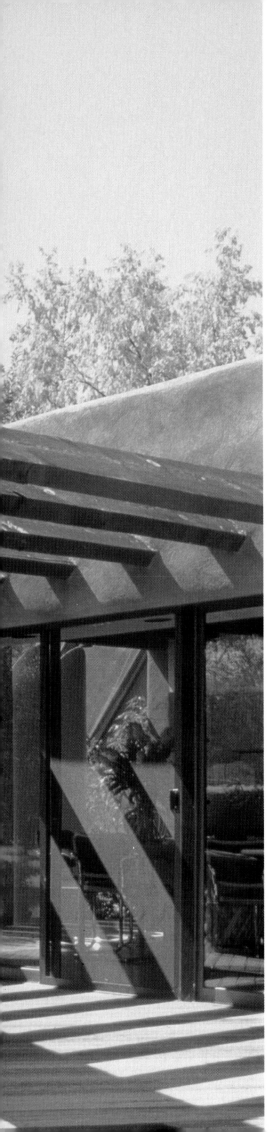

Left: *This unique design incorporates patio, porch, and pergola. Open-air roof beams invite hanging plants and cast a dramatic graphic design on the buildings and sidewalk.*

Right: *Casual furnishings and the warm embrace of adobe are all that's needed for a successful patio. But barrels used as planters, a brick floor, and vigas overhead add interest to the simple setting.*

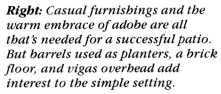

Left: *The portal in Old Town Albuquerque leads to shops and galleries in the city's historic section.*

159

Left: Simple, rounded vigas define the form and structure of this portal. *The unusual round lintel adds to the woodsy feeling of the design and blends nicely with the relaxed, natural landscaping.*

Above: The architecture and natural-wood patio furnishings are simple and organic, allowing an uncluttered experience of the pristine view of the Sangre de Cristo Mountains.

Above: This ultramodern variation on the portal *provides cool shade on a hot, sunny day. Its concrete and steel superstructure and fabric sunshades are a dramatic contrast to the stucco house, but its design and function are completely consistent with the most important elements of Santa Fe design.*

161

JARDÍNES

GARDENS

During much of the year, Santa Fe's mild climate encourages people to stay outdoors day and night. Almost every house has at least one comfortable outdoor living space that makes the most of this terrific weather. Days are usually warm and sunny, so most *jardínes* offer a shaded arbor, patio, or *portal* as a shelter from the bright sun. But nights are cool, and an outdoor fireplace or radiant heat from adobe walls is always welcome. Screen porches are unnecessary in New Mexico because there aren't many insects, but the steadily blowing wind needs to be tamed by walls or other enclosures. Many of these walls are treated much like walls inside a house: They are hung with *ristras* and fitted with *bancos*. Water is highly prized in New Mexico, and many garden designs include a small fountain, a goldfish pond, or a meditation pool.

Most visitors to New Mexico enjoy the climate but find that the semiarid landscape looks somewhat barren. If they stay around long enough, they learn to recognize the beauty of the Southwest's particular natural palette, which ranges from the pearlescence of yucca blossoms in sunlight to subtle shades of green and gray where mesquite and prickly pear cactus blend into blue grama and buffalo grasses. On rolling hills and mesas dotted by piñon, cedar, and juniper trees, dramatic earth colors—coral, salmon, and lavender—peek through the evergreens. In fall sage blooms cadmium yellow, and fields are dotted with purple asters and wild sunflowers. In summer bluebonnets, blue flax, and Rocky Mountain columbines contrast with the dazzling crimson, scarlet, and violet of Indian paintbrush and penstemons.

New Mexican gardeners know that left alone the thin, sandy soil of the high desert can produce a rainbow of glorious color. But attempting to garden in the desert can lead to disastrous results. The best way to assure success is to choose native plants and sun-loving flowers, including snapdragons, geraniums, poppies, and hollyhocks. Walls that control the wind and terraces that hold water in the soil are essential to a successful garden. Lawns require steady watering and extensive care, so many Santa Fe gardeners keep them small or dispense with them altogether, preferring a brick patio or a cultivated field of wildflowers and native grasses.

A garden in Santa Fe can be a welcome oasis from the desert, a carefully orchestrated display of native plants and flowering perennials, or a natural stand of cacti and wildflowers. But New Mexico gardens have one thing in common. The peace and harmony that you encounter in these *jardínes* comes not from the gardener's effort to control nature but from a heartfelt recognition of our dependence on nature. Every Santa Fe gardener looks to the sky and the hills for inspiration and learns to work with limited resources to create beauty that is in harmony with this magnificent natural setting.

Right: The serene vista of a formal garden overlooking Santa Fe is broken by a rustic pole ladder. Snapdragons and petunias fill beds along a curving earthen wall that defines the view.

Left: Santa Fe art dealer Forrest Fenn created this sumptuous sculpture garden at his compound. Lazy willow branches overhang a pond lined with river rocks and native Southwestern plants. Across a bluegrass lawn, sculptures by Southwestern artists are frozen in time and space.

Right: Overgrown arbors, once associated with old ranches and Victorian mansions, are making a comeback at country houses around Santa Fe.

Right: Don Gregorio Crespin sold this house with its "lands and apricot tree" in 1747 to Bartolomé Marquez. Located just across the Santa Fe River from the Plaza in the Barrio de Analco residential district, this house boasts one of the city's finest gardens. The entire yard seems to revolve around the magnificent grandfather tree.

Left: The romance of an evening spent on a Santa Fe patio is unmistakable. Earth-colored walls glow golden, amber, and russet from the embers in the bell-shaped fireplace. Built-in bancos *and Mexican* equipale *furniture encourage guests to linger over dinner and enjoy the fire.*

Left: Only a ribbon of salmon-colored adobe wall separates a gorgeous, cultivated Santa Fe garden from a wild forest of century-old trees. A mountain-flower garden blossoms with deep violet, sage green, lavender, and cadmium yellow.

Right: This secluded Santa Fe courtyard offers more than a refreshing view of lush green plants. A Copernican sundial, a wall nicho of Madonna and child, a millstone, and an inspired collection of unusual rocks bring a decidedly human element into the garden.

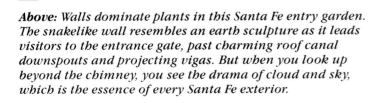

Above: Walls dominate plants in this Santa Fe entry garden. The snakelike wall resembles an earth sculpture as it leads visitors to the entrance gate, past charming roof canal downspouts and projecting vigas. But when you look up beyond the chimney, you see the drama of cloud and sky, which is the essence of every Santa Fe exterior.

Above: Giant trees shroud this Corrales house in a verdant midsummer cloak. Wild grasses flourish uncultivated, and the setting is reminiscent of a colonial hacienda on the northern frontier.

Right: The angled flagstone steps, flat roof, and square lines of the building give this garden a distinctly Aztecan feeling. It is monumental, but a bounty of blooming flowers lines the path and promises in time to soften the garden's formality.

Right: Potted geraniums, rose bushes, and blazing orange California poppies sing in the clear New Mexican sunlight. Built-in bancos along the high walls of this garden face a central fountain where friends gather in the cool twilight.

Left: A fountain and water maze in the patio of the School of American Research is monumental despite its small physical scale. The scene sparks the imagination with the image of a temple dedicated to a long-forgotten deity; the rock and adobe forms seem to have symbolic meanings that no one remembers.

Right: Behind the high walls of this house on Santa Fe's Canyon Road, a small garden pool—a wishing well perhaps—is the essence of tranquility. The pool perfectly balances the steps that are made with natural boulders and stones. It is obviously a treasured spot.

Left: *Random, loose-fit stonework offsets the smooth mass of plastered adobe walls, making a gracious transition from the entrance portal to a small patio to the lower tier of walled flower beds into the yard.*

Right: *Mountain, wood, and water are celebrated in this classic garden. Architecture is reduced to its most fundamental expression: a roof supported by corbeled columns. This frames the natural setting, emphasizing its importance.*

Left: *When architect Bob Peters remodeled this house, he preserved the inner courtyard, giving it a light baffle ceiling to filter the sunlight. By adding wooden grids to strong pine columns and lintels, Peters evokes both Southwest and Japanese design themes.*

Above: *Towering poplar and spruce trees break the rhythm of a sequence of planter walls, steps, and angled horizontal vectors of wood and wall. This dramatic design is by Studio Arquitectura.*

171

SANTA FE ARTS

Here's a quick lesson in Santa Fe design: Choose furniture that is generously scaled and upholstered in textured tones of desert colors. Add a Mexican tile floor and a white plaster fireplace. Then let in lots of clear, bright sunlight during the day and bring in soft, gentle light at night. This is the basic framework for a warm, sensuous room, but it lacks the ingredients that will make it unmistakably Santa Fe. The room needs objects made in the Southwest that speak of the purple hills, the clean desert air, and the rich Pueblo and colonial past. Pueblo pots, Hopi kachina dolls, Apache baskets, Hispanic folk art, paintings or lithographs by Santa Fe artists, tin lamps, and any other examples of Southwestern arts and crafts are essential elements of Santa Fe design. But imagination is the key to arranging objects in a Santa Fe interior. Without imagination the most carefully planned and expensive room is lifeless. A touch of whimsy, a hint of spontaneous good humor, or a quick nod to history gives spirit to a room.

Objects made in Santa Fe bring a breath of Santa Fe air to any room, anywhere in the world. Artists who live and work in Santa Fe are naturally affected by the clarity of the atmosphere, the high altitude, and the open spaces. There is room to breathe here, and this openness is reflected in the works of art that are made in the Southwest. These objects give back something of the person who made them. They bear "the mark of the hand, the mark of the tool," as Santa Fe architect Bruce Davis says. The potter's hand is evident in softly colored handmade tiles as well as traditional Pueblo pots. The weaver or basket maker may include a slight, purposeful irregularity of line to add an organic fidelity to a rug or basket. But the work is never forced or deliberately crude; it is simply in tune with the rhythms of the landscape. The tinsmith or woodcarver may remember the long history of his craft and the ways the necessities of life in Nuevo México changed how objects are made. The jeweler looks out across the purple-shaded hills and sees not only the source of her raw materials but may also find the design for a new bracelet. The painter may capture the way light falls through golden aspen leaves or turn inward to express the way it feels to live close to the earth as people do in Santa Fe. It's the human touch that distinguishes the best Santa Fe arts and crafts. There is an orderly calm in objects that reflects the beautiful place in which they are made.

Right: Design by architects Johnson, Nestor, Mortier, and Rodriguez

BASKETS

Above: These Apache ollas, or storage baskets, were woven in the early 1900s. The animal pictured in the decorative motifs is probably a dog, since dogs were traditionally portrayed with their tails up. The crosses represent the four directions that are sacred to the Apaches.

Right: This Chemehuevi basket features a design of birds. Because this olla is highly decorated, it was probably made for sale to tourists, but even so, it is a stunning work of art. The basket is made of willow; the black birds are woven of devil's claw, and their eyes are probably yucca root.

Long before they had learned to make pottery, the Anasazi advanced the art of basket weaving to its highest level. They made bowls, jugs, trays, and other containers in many sizes and shapes using a technique that bound coil weaving with splints. Vessels could be woven so tightly that they were able to hold water. The Anasazi even cooked in baskets, using hot rocks to heat water to cook dried beans.

Since the advent of clay pots, baskets have been used primarily as large, durable containers and have not needed to be so tightly woven that they are watertight. When the Apaches and Navajos arrived in the Southwest, they developed their own basket-making traditions. The Hopis continue to weave colorful coiled plaques and baskets for ceremonial purposes such as weddings. The Papagos of southern Arizona, who are descendants of the prehistoric Hohokam, produce large numbers of excellent baskets, and the Western Apaches of Arizona, the Jicarilla Apaches of northern New Mexico, and the Mescalero Apaches of southern New Mexico maintain high artistic standards and produce superb baskets.

Above: *This* olla *was made in the 1880s. The basket's design is Western Apache.*

Above: *This finely woven Yavapai basket is not especially heavy-duty and was probably made to be traded to Pueblos to use for storing grain. The* olla, *which has a design of men and animals, was probably made in the early 1900s.*

Above: *Classic Yavapai baskets, like this one, are distinguished by positive/negative triangles, with a design of crosses also reversing to positive/negative.*

Above: *Basket trays, or shallow bowls, were used for gathering saguaro fruit and other foods. Once filled, the baskets were carried on the head. This kind of basket was also used for parching and winnowing (tossing grain into the air to separate the seed from the chaff). These Apache trays show a strong Yavapai influence. The basket in the center is polychrome, and yucca root was used in the red areas.*

Above: *The figures in this design include horses, men, and other creatures. Horses are traditionally woven with their tails pointing down to distinguish them from dogs. The Apache Star, which is the dominant design motif of this basket, is a direct reference to the sacred four directions.*

Above: *This prehistoric coiled basket from the Mojave District of western Arizona was possibly a cooking vessel in which dried beans and water were heated with hot rocks.*

Left: *This polychrome Apache* olla *features an unusual composition of male and female figures holding baskets.*

Above: *These Pima baskets were probably made around 1930. There is a basic structural difference between a Pima basket and an Apache basket, even though both are made of willow and devil's claw. The foundation of a Pima basket is a bundle of grass; the foundation of an Apache basket is three willow rods. The patterns are also different, and Pima baskets are characterized by geometric, repetitive, swirling patterns.*

Above: *The colors in this polychrome Chemehuevi basket are unique. Instead of the usual black, tan, and red, the basket is black, tan, and golden orange because the weaver chose to use juncus. This reed grows mostly in southern California and was difficult to obtain.*

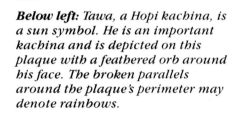

Below left: *Tawa, a Hopi kachina, is a sun symbol. He is an important kachina and is depicted on this plaque with a feathered orb around his face. The broken parallels around the plaque's perimeter may denote rainbows.*

Above: *In a traditional Navajo wedding ceremony, this wedding tray would have been filled with cornmeal. The participants each put a finger in the center of the tray and draw a line through the cornmeal straight out to its edge, attempting to trace the line in the tray's design, which is covered up by the cornmeal.*

Above: *Crow Mother is one of the most powerful Hopi kachinas. She rules over the bean sprout ceremony, the central point in the kachina cycle. She also presides over initiation ceremonies in the kivas. Crow Mother is often shown on plaques.*

Below: *These contemporary baskets were made to be sold to collectors, but their shapes are traditional. The basket on the lower right is a Navajo wedding basket; top center is a Hopi tray with a Corn Maiden kachina design. The four miniatures are Tohono O'odham horsehair baskets, and the Pima basket is the one with a four-petal squash design.*

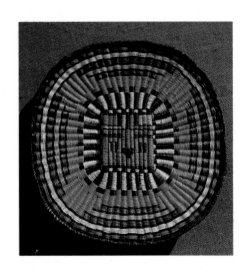

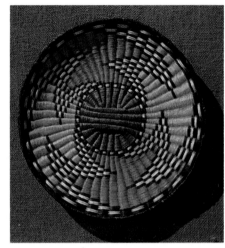

Above: *These Hopi baskets are used for a variety of purposes. The three plaques include a butterfly and a kachina design. Two of the utility baskets at the right are sifters; the other is a painted* piki *tray, used to carry the paper-thin blue-corn bread of the Hopis.*

Above right: *The pure exuberance of its design distinguishes this Hopi wicker plaque. This kind of basket is used in dances or as a gift or prize.*

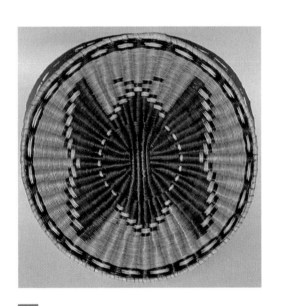

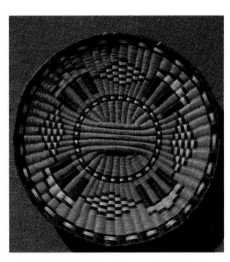

Above: *A deep-blue butterfly forms the central design of this Hopi plaque, woven during the 1930s. The blue has bled into the surrounding area beautifully, softening its appearance.*

Above: *This plaque was made in one of the oldest Hopi villages, Oraibi, in 1969. The pattern may symbolize rain clouds emanating from each of the four directions. Clouds are frequently depicted as speckled to indicate that they are full of rain.*

POTTERY

It is difficult to imagine a Santa Fe interior without a Pueblo *olla*, or ceremonial pottery vessel, sitting in a *nicho* or displayed on the mantel. Like other prehistoric Indians in the Southwest, Pueblo potters have been creating pots for everyday and ceremonial use for more than a thousand years. When the Spanish and later the Americans arrived in Santa Fe, these newcomers recognized the beauty and utility of Indian pottery and encouraged its continued production. Today there are many traditional and innovative pottery studios in town and throughout the pueblos.

Each group of Pueblos developed colors and styles of pottery. Hopi, Zuni, Laguna, and Acoma potters make vessels with black-and-white motifs and also polychrome (black, white, and red) painted designs. The Hopi potter Nampeyo, who worked at the turn of the century, evolved dynamic, interlocked swirling designs. Zuni *ollas* sometimes show deer and bears with red heart lines. Acoma and Laguna pots often feature bold flower designs in polychrome, embellished with scrolls and birds.

Santa Clara, San Juan, and San Ildefonso pueblos all boast famous potters whose work sells for thousands of dollars. Santa Clara pottery has highly polished black or red surfaces, and carved relief designs. San Ildefonso was the home of María Martínez. Along with her husband, Julian, she made distinctive gloss-black vessels with black-matte designs. Their grandson Tony Da makes pots that combine this technique with polishing, incising, and embedding turquoise and carved fetish figures.

In many pueblos every phase of making pots, from digging the clay to the final polishing, is still done in the old way. Pots are built without a wheel, using the coil method. Pueblo potters are able to achieve remarkably thin-walled vessels that are accurately round. Once they have dried, pots are carefully fired using bark and other materials to achieve the desired results.

Many of the potters working in Santa Fe today use another traditional process, raku, which requires low heat and less equipment than high-fired ceramics. It also relies on such natural materials as straw to create color variations during the cooling process. These potters favor simple forms that can often stand alone as sculpture. The glaze and texture of the pieces support their visual impact.

Dinnerware and casseroles are high-fired in conventional kilns for durability. This process yields deep, vivid colors and a surface that is impervious to liquids or grease. These brightly colored dishes are a perfect complement to New Mexican cooking.

Santa Fe pottery is now, as it has been for hundreds of generations, an important and respected craft. Pots are carefully crafted to be displayed or used daily. The potter's work is basic to life. As Priscilla Hoback, whose teaching has inspired many other potters, has said, "It's the human thing to do."

Right: This striking nicho *is embellished with a bird motif that is a classic Pueblo pottery design. The* nicho *displays fine old pots from the upper Rio Grande Valley of New Mexico.*

Above: *This collection of Pueblo pottery from the Heard Museum in Phoenix, Arizona, includes historic polychrome (three-color) vessels, such as the Pohoge storage vessels in the back, as well as one of María Martínez's black pots in the front.*

Below: *Zia Pueblo pottery designs are slightly different from those of neighboring western New Mexico pueblos. Potters from Zia usually cover the entire surface of their pots with designs, leaving very little background. This fine jar, made in about 1905, is typical of Zia pottery, but it also shows the hand of the particular potter who made it in its precise cross-hatching.*

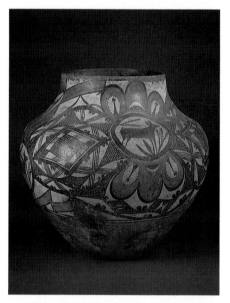

Above: *Cochiti Pueblo has long been one of the major pottery centers in New Mexico. These distinctive storage vessels and canteen were made there during the late 1800s. The unusual canteen has a narrow neck, two lug handles, and a raised frog design—a delightful combination of utility and artistic expression.*

Above: *These two pots from Zuni Pueblo were crafted around 1900. The flowerlike medallion may reflect a Spanish influence. The deer figures with a life arrow running through their mouths are Zuni icons.*

Left: This large Zia polychrome jar was probably crafted around the turn of the century. The banded design is typical except that in this instance there is an additional band around the shoulder of the pot.

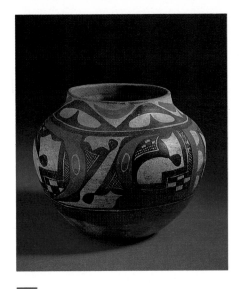

Above: This polychrome jar dates from the late 1800s. It is from Santa Ana Pueblo in western New Mexico. This pueblo does not produce much pottery today, but historically pots made in Santa Ana are distinguished by the boldness of their designs.

Left: This Tewa polychrome vessel has a feather motif and is unusual because it has a lid, indicating that it may be a later piece that was specially ordered with a lid.

Right: These pots were made by Nampeyo and her family. Nampeyo is responsible for the revival of the ancient Sikyatki style of pottery among Hopi potters. The large jar at the top left was made by Nampeyo around 1900.

183

Right: San Ildefonso potter Barbara Gonzáles is a great-granddaughter of María Martínez. Like many of María's other descendants, she carries on the family tradition of making fine ceramic pieces that are variations on age-old themes.

Above: The legendary potter María of San Ildefonso crafted her vessels using the coil method rather than a wheel. Engineers who calibrated them were amazed to find that the pots were flawlessly circular. María's son, Popovi Da, painted many of her polychrome pieces, including the plate shown here.

Above: Hopi potters in northeastern Arizona have access to lovely buff-colored clay that is unavailable in the upper Rio Grande Valley of New Mexico. These disk-shaped pots were decorated with Sikyatki motifs by potter Mike Hawley.

Right: The Sikyatki design of these contemporary pots by Mike Hawley is historically correct. The revival of this ancient design style was begun by Nampeyo, who studied pot shards from the ruined village of Sikyatki.

Left: Lois Gutierrez De La Cruz of Santa Clara used ancient design themes for these polychrome pots. The motifs of the pot in the center hearken back to the prehistoric Basket Maker culture of southern Arizona.

Above: María Martínez of San Ildefonso was the most influential Native American potter of modern times. During her long life, she produced a large body of classically elegant work, notably the black pots for which she is famous. This polychrome piece, with a plumed serpent around its neck, may have been painted by her husband Julian.

Right: The feather motif on this polychrome vessel is proportioned with contemporary boldness, which is carried farther by the dynamic, syncopated design around the lower band. Blue Corn of San Ildefonso, who created this piece in 1976, is among the most famous living potters.

Above: These contemporary pots are typical of those being produced at Acoma, the "pueblo in the sky," which is built atop a high mesa in western New Mexico. Zuni and Zia artists also produce pots with similar motifs.

185

Left: *Al Qöyawayma's distinctive art is all his own. Shaping his pots in the tradition of his ancestors, he then applies raised sculptural elements. His themes, such as corn and the Kokopelli flute player shown here, arise from his Hopi culture, but Qöyawayma employs them in a uniquely contemporary fashion.*

Left : *The small pot on the left is a contemporary piece in the style created by Grace Medicine Flower and Joseph Lonewolf. These precisely etched, meticulously polished vessels are frequently executed in miniature. The larger pot shows another modern innovation, the use of turquoise inlay.*

Above: *This regal vase by Al Qöyawayma is executed in the buff-colored clay unique to Hopi pottery. The image carved in bas-relief shows a Corn Maiden kachina dancer.*

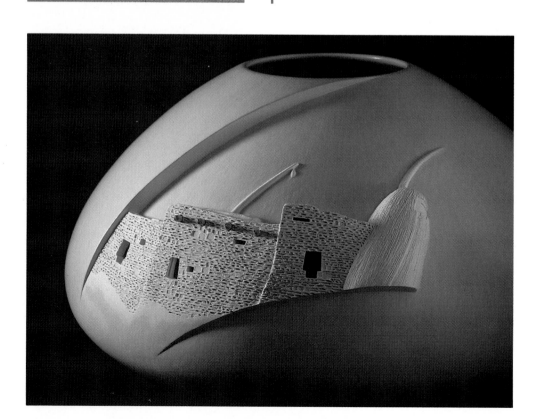

Right: *Potter Al Qöyawayma uses the vessel itself as a landscape and embellishes it with bas-reliefs of Hopi architecture. His swirling composition evokes the highly refined ceremonial customs of the potter's Hopi culture.*

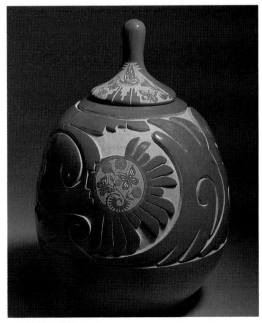

Above: Ancient pot shards reveal that Pueblo potters have long painted designs on their pots. The practice of carving lines into the clay is a recent innovation. When he made these pots, Hopi artist Thomas Polacca combined old and new techniques and imagery.

Above right: Santa Clara potter Grace Medicine Flower is known for her intricate carving and her beautifully drawn natural images, which are often colored in such nontraditional shades as blue.

Left: These three Tewa pots abstract traditional images in such a way that they become dynamic modern statements about historic design themes.

Right: This beautifully burnished redware bowl takes its shape from a melon.

Right: Potters from Acoma Pueblo are renowned for the stunning perfection of their geometric designs. Rose Chino Garcia made the pot on the left; her sister, Grace Chino, made the two other pots. Their work develops motifs associated with Mimbres pottery.

Left: Rose Gonzáles follows the tradition of her great-grandmother, María of San Ildefonso, in the fluid design of these richly carved and burnished red and black pots.

Left: María Martínez crafted classically proportioned pots with traditional Tewa motifs carved and etched into their surfaces.

Right: This group of pots by Dorothy Torivio of Acoma Pueblo is a masterful expression of her art. Torivio uses clay with black and white glazes to produce a meditative, cellular geometry of kaleidoscopic grace.

Below: Dorothy Torivio created this pot of almost surreal perfection. It was purchased by the Albuquerque International Airport for its excellent collection of New Mexico art that is showcased in the terminal building for passengers to view and enjoy.

Below: In her long and illustrious lifetime, María Martínez produced a wide variety of pots, working alone or with her husband, Julian, or her son, Popovi Da, who sometimes painted polychrome pieces. But her hallmark image was the simple black pot. This one features a bird design, which was somewhat unusual for María.

Left: *This variation on the storyteller theme depicts a bear with a cluster of playful cubs. The skillful adaptation of the traditional red, black, and white polychrome gives this contemporary piece a festive look.*

Below: *These three black pots represent one of the finest New Mexican craft traditions, while the storyteller figure is a delightful modern departure made popular by Helen Cordero of Cochiti Pueblo. Storytellers are an interpretation in clay of the Pueblo oral-history tradition. The symmetrical placement of the listening children makes this piece particularly charming.*

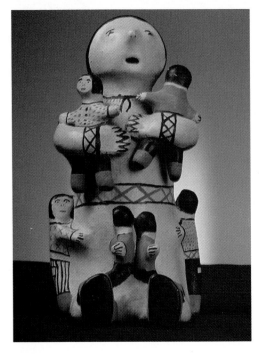

Above: *Aurelia Suina made this Cochiti storyteller in 1975, but the figure has a delightfully primitive quality.*

190

Above: Rose Chino Garcia made this intricately designed Acoma jar in 1984. Working within a tradition of expanded geometric design, she achieves a remarkable range of individual expression.

Above right: Zuni potter Anderson Peynetsa combines Acoma geometric and Zuni figurative motifs in this traditionally shaped graceful vessel. The deer has a life arrow running into its mouth, signifying the breath of life.

Above: The Pueblo people of the Rio Grande Valley and parts of western New Mexico and northeastern Arizona have been making clay vessels for more than a thousand years. The few surviving intact examples, as well as millions of pot shards, point to an ongoing concern with esthetics as well as utility.

Right: This classic redware pot by María has an unusual shape, reflecting the ability of this potter to transcend even her own distinctive style.

Left: *Santa Fe's close association with Pueblo pottery has made it an internationally known center for fine ceramics, and artists with many different cultural backgrounds now show their work in galleries here. One of these potters, Avra Leodas, created this large vessel. Its subtle shape and rough texture contrast dramatically with its smooth interior.*

Left: *These classically shaped pots by María and her son, Popovi Da, are so highly burnished that they have the appearance of gunmetal. The slight texture of the clay lends an opalescent, earthy richness to their clear reflections.*

Right: *Potter Leah Elizabeth Parsons works with pure abstract form, composing her vessels as sculpture. The medallion element on this pot relates subtly to Zuni fetishes that are sometimes applied to contemporary Pueblo pottery, while the shaded stripe glows like a neon light at dusk.*

Above: *Richard Zane Smith is a potter of Wyandot descent. His ancestors were not pottery-making people, and Smith works outside the Pueblo tradition. His surface decorations almost resemble computer art, and the shape and texture of his pots are much like those of Apache* olla *baskets.*

Above: *This starkly elegant vessel by Jon Middlemiss resonates with themes from ancient and modern Pueblo pottery: It has Mimbres black-and-white simplicity of color, Acoma geometric perfection, and the syncopation of Hopi Sikyatki motifs.*

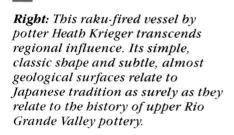

Right: *This raku-fired vessel by potter Heath Krieger transcends regional influence. Its simple, classic shape and subtle, almost geological surfaces relate to Japanese tradition as surely as they relate to the history of upper Rio Grande Valley pottery.*

TEXTILES

Most of the rugs used in Santa Fe design are woven by Navajos in New Mexico and Arizona. Most blankets are woven by Spanish families in northern New Mexico, particularly in the area around Chimayo and El Valle, just north of Santa Fe. Spanish craftspeople also make flowery *colcha* embroidered tapestries.

When the Navajos arrived in the Four Corners area six centuries ago, they began gradually to assimilate many aspects of Pueblo culture. They borrowed some ceremonial and religious practices, and also learned the craft of weaving.

Before 1863 when the U.S. Army removed the Navajos from their beloved homeland in the Four Corners and forced them to settle at Bosque Redondo, Navajo rug designs had evolved from simple stripes to include terraced zigzags and diamonds. At Bosque Redondo the army issued Hispanic Rio Grande blankets to the Navajos. These Hispanic blankets were heavily influenced by the textiles from Saltillo that had been brought to New Mexico by the Spanish colonists. The Hispanic blankets featured a large central diamond motif. When the Navajos returned to their homeland in 1868, Navajo weavers immediately incorporated the Saltillo diamond into their weaving.

Navajo weavers tend to be eclectic in their tastes, and a large variety of styles of rugs is available. Some recognizable patterns and rugs are highly collectible. These include historic chief's blankets woven before 1900, the Ganado Red style of weaving encouraged by that turn-of-the-century trading post, Two Gray Hills tapestries, storm-pattern rugs, pictorial rugs, and sand-painting designs.

The Hispanic Rio Grande style of weaving developed alongside Navajo weaving. Early Navajo and Hispanic blankets have simple horizontal stripe designs. But after 1830 Hispanic blankets often have a dominant central medallion or diamond motif that was influenced by serapes imported from Saltillo. In the late nineteenth century, families in the high mountain villages of El Valle and Chimayo developed their own distinctive weaving designs. El Valle blankets display radiant stars and zigzag stripe motifs; Chimayo blankets have stylized thunderbird designs.

In Chimayo master weavers at the Ortega Weaving Shop as well as Theresa Archuleta-Sagel, Maria Vergara-Wilson, and Juanita Jaramillo-Lavadie create exquisite work. In Rio Arriba county an innovative cooperative, Tierra Wools, is breeding long-haired merino sheep, a Spanish breed that had practically died out in New Mexico. Tierra Wools is also training a new generation of Hispanic weavers to meet the growing demand for Rio Grande textiles.

Right: Hopi weaver Ramona Sakiestewa expresses her contemporary vision in traditional ways. Sakiestewa's meticulously loomed textiles have abstract motifs that echo the style and pattern of chief's blankets and Rio Grande serapes.

Left: The Santa Fe Indian Market, which is held on the Plaza in mid-August, is a major event for Native American weavers and other craftspeople.

Above: The Navajo weavers of Teec Nos Pos, located in the Four Corners area of northeastern Arizona, are famed for the complexity of their designs. Their rugs have wide, patterned borders and many small elements arranged in intricate patterns. Feathers are the design motif of the center panel in this rug.

Above: Navajo chief's blankets were woven in the nineteenth century. They are characterized by a pattern of diamonds placed within stripes. The swastika design in the middle of the flattened diamonds is an ancient motif, which also appears in the designs of many other cultures around the world.

197

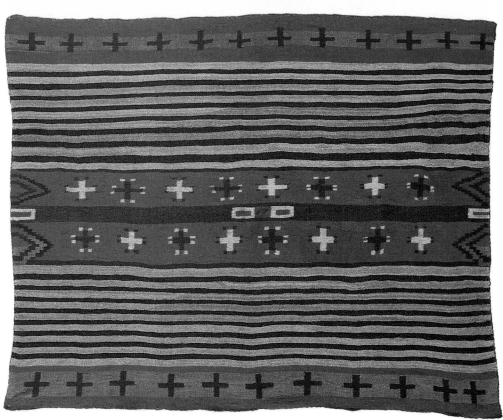

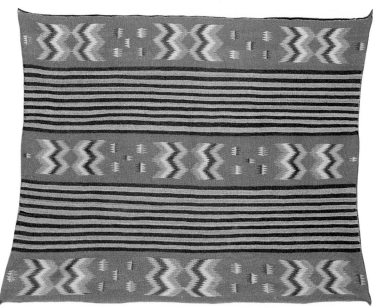

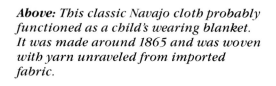

Above: This classic Navajo cloth probably functioned as a child's wearing blanket. It was made around 1865 and was woven with yarn unraveled from imported fabric.

Above: This Navajo cloth from the mid-nineteenth century is a woman's shoulder blanket, characterized by two bands of narrow stripes. The equilateral cross signifies the four directions.

Left: This man's shoulder blanket was made between 1865 and 1870. The piece is tightly woven from hand-spun yarn. It has retained much of its original color.

Left: The fine weaving in this piece, with its serrated patterns, was probably made possible by the use of Germantown yarn. The striped bands interspersed between the three patterned areas identify it as a woman's shoulder blanket.

Right: This chief's blanket made with Germantown yarn was woven around 1890. Its design is unusual: All the diamonds are connected, and four pictorial elements, weaving combs that resemble little paintbrushes, have been incorporated.

Right: Early Spanish and Navajo weaving have many similarities, but Spanish pieces, like this one that was made during the mid-nineteenth century in northern New Mexico, can usually be distinguished from Navajo work by their pattern of stripes with no surrounding border.

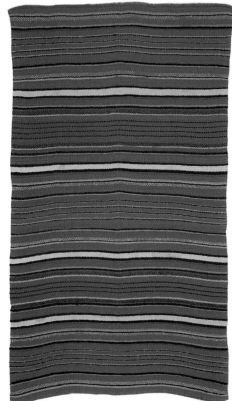

Below: Woven textiles made by Spanish settlers of New Mexico are known as Rio Grande textiles, because the Spanish villages were located in the river basin. Rio Grande designs almost always incorporate stripes. This piece of cloth may have been influenced by colcha embroidery. It was woven on a New Mexican-made horizontal loom with fixed heddles that was operated by a foot mechanism.

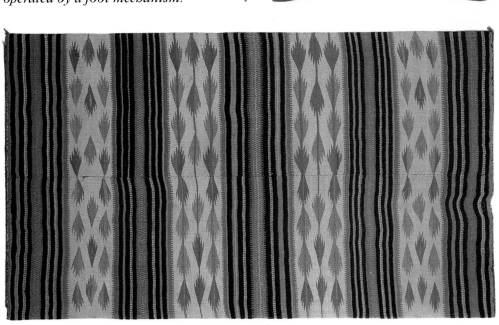

Above: This contemporary Navajo rug by Kalley Keams Musial is made in a traditional saddle-blanket style, but the weaver has chosen to combine a twilled pattern and a tapestry motif in an interesting variation.

199

Left: *In Santa Fe fine Indian rugs and blankets are often hung on the wall where they can be enjoyed for their artistic merit. This piece relates beautifully to the other design elements in the room.*

Below left: *The Two Gray Hills Trading Post in northeastern Arizona was instrumental in encouraging weavers in the surrounding area to use wool in its natural colors. Instead of dyeing yarn, colors from black, brown, gray, or white sheep were spun separately. Two Gray Hills weavers are also known for the exceptionally close, fine texture of their work. This is an early-twentieth-century piece.*

Below right: *Victoria Keoni created this Burnt Water textile with its complex geometric pattern. The weaving style originated in the early 1970s and uses wool yarn hand carded and spun, and dyed with plant dyes in slightly unusual color combinations. Burnt Water rugs are reminiscent of Oriental carpets.*

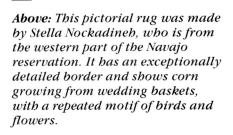

Above: This pictorial rug was made by Stella Nockadineh, who is from the western part of the Navajo reservation. It has an exceptionally detailed border and shows corn growing from wedding baskets, with a repeated motif of birds and flowers.

Above: Indian rugs are known by the specific area from which they come. Two Gray Hills, on the Navajo reservation, is the most famous and possibly the most sought after style of rugs. The colors are all natural, just as they come from the sheep, and the weaving is extraordinarily fine. This tapestry was made by sisters Rose Ann Lee and Barbara Teller Ornelas.

Right: This detail of one of Victoria Keoni's fine contemporary Wide Ruins rugs shows her meticulous use of pattern, texture, and soft-toned plant dyes. The rug in its entirety is absolutely symmetrical, with pattern equally distributed to the selvages.

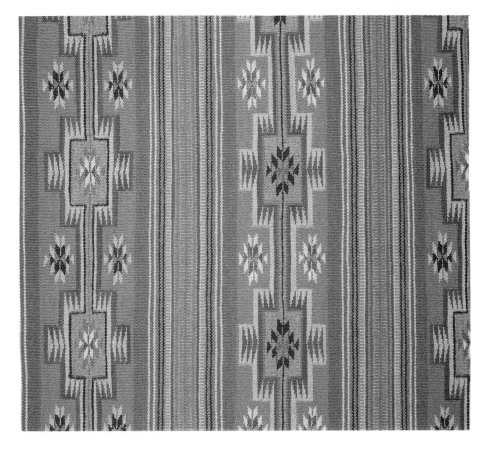

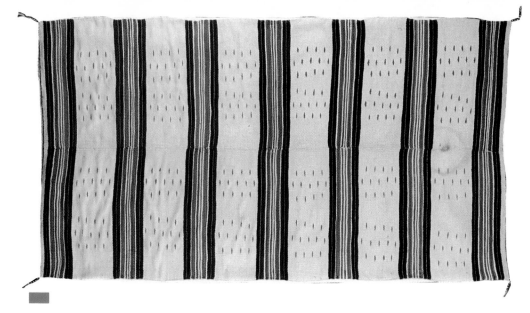

Above: This Rio Grande blanket probably dates from 1820 to 1850. It is made of cotton instead of wool and was woven on a narrow Spanish horizontal loom, since it has a seam up the middle.

Right: This pictorial rug surrounds symbols of the United States with the kind of geometric border often used in Navajo fabric designs.

Above: This mid-nineteenth century piece was probably cochineal dyed. This red dye is made from the dried bodies of female cochineal insects, which feed on cactus.

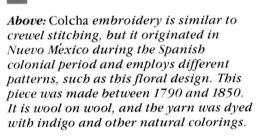

Above: This beautiful old Navajo chief's blanket was woven from yarn colored with dyes made from plants and insects.

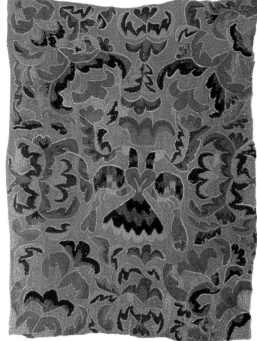

Above: Colcha *embroidery is similar to crewel stitching, but it originated in Nuevo México during the Spanish colonial period and employs different patterns, such as this floral design. This piece was made between 1790 and 1850. It is wool on wool, and the yarn was dyed with indigo and other natural colorings.*

Above: This contemporary Navajo pictorial rug organizes scenes of day-to-day life into broad stripes.

Left: *A technique known as wedge weaving gives this piece highly valued slanted stripes and a wavy border. To achieve this result, the warp was pulled hard to one side and then to the other. This blanket was probably made during the 1870s.*

JEWELRY

Within sight of Santa Fe, there is a low range of piñon-dotted hills, which is filled with the precious and semiprecious minerals used to make traditional and contemporary Southwestern jewelry. There is a working turquoise mine in these hills, but much of the silver and turquoise used by Santa Fe jewelers is mined in other parts of the Southwest.

Before the Pueblos and Navajos learned silversmithing from Hispanic colonists, they had made boldly designed jewelry from carved stones and shells. Many contemporary Santa Fe jewelers base their designs on this prehistoric jewelry. Fetish necklaces are made of carved stone animals strung as beads. The multicolored geology of the region is reflected in the arrangement of the stones.

Each village developed a distinctive style of silver jewelry, and most contemporary Indian jewelry looks like the fine old pawn pieces that inspired it. Other jewelers who work in silver have added such nontraditional minerals as jasper, agate, coral, lapis lazuli, and malachite to their handsome compositions.

The exuberance of Santa Fe is interpreted in jewelry with incisive wit and high elegance. The best examples of Santa Fe jewelry successfully bring together themes from the surrounding high desert and mountains, Indian and Spanish motifs, and contemporary trends.

Above: Old pawn jewelry, including a squash blossom necklace, spills from an antique Papago-Pima basket. The rug is a Two Gray Hills design.

Right: Navajo jeweler Harvey Begay interprets ancient themes in a stylized manner. His work has an element of Art Deco design.

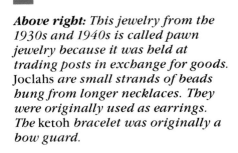

Above: Ben Nighthorse, a Northern Cheyenne, incorporates designs from pottery and other Native American crafts into his exquisitely wrought jewelry.

Above right: This jewelry from the 1930s and 1940s is called pawn jewelry because it was held at trading posts in exchange for goods. Joclahs *are small strands of beads hung from longer necklaces. They were originally used as earrings. The* ketoh *bracelet was originally a bow guard.*

Above: The necklace displayed on the log is called a squash blossom. The sandcast bracelet with flat-stone channel inlay work is from Zuni Pueblo. The lower bracelet is Navajo and was made in the 1930s.

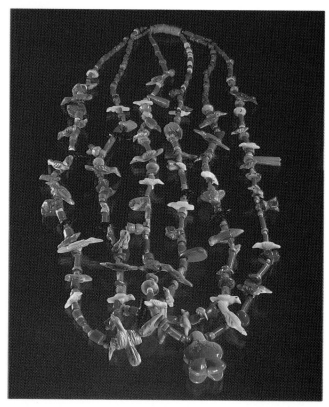

Left: Many Native American silversmiths now use modern designs in their work. These abstract and figurative pieces show the adaptability of Navajo and Pueblo ancestral images, including the Corn Maiden and the bear with a traditional life arrow coming into its mouth.

Below: Leekya Deyuse, who made this necklace, was the finest fetish carver at Zuni Pueblo during the 1930s. At that time birds and other animals were beginning to be carved in a more lifelike fashion than earlier fetishes, which were often natural rock formations that only hinted at an animal form. The elongated red beads that separate the carved animals in this necklace are unusual.

Above: "The Drop Dead Necklace," the name of this piece, is a registered trademark of an anonymous jeweler who exhibits her work at Santa Fe East.

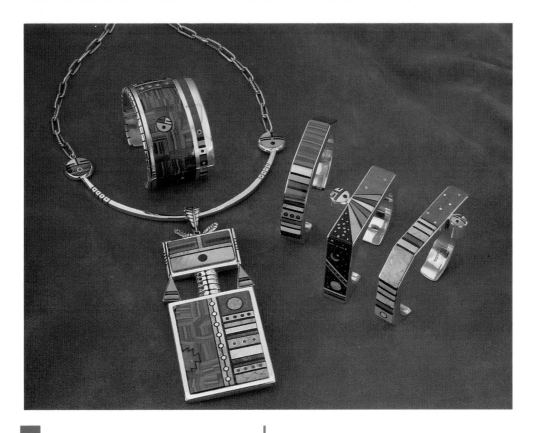

Above: *Jeweler Jesse Monongya works with geometric abstract designs that incorporate traditional Pueblo images. There are little Sun kachina faces on the bracelets, and a highly abstracted full kachina figure forms the pendant of the necklace.*

Left: *Navajo artist James Little sets traditional stones, such as turquoise and coral, in gold rather than silver. This necklace made with Nevada Blue turquoise represents the male and female Yei gods of the Navajo. The bracelet, set with Burnham turquoise, tells a symbolic story.*

Above right: *This modern bead necklace was designed and crafted by jewelers Allan Edgar and Judith Young. In form, color, and composition, it epitomizes Santa Fe design through its Native American elements combined with precious materials and international references.*

Right: *This striking piece of jewelry by Patricia Brady and Richard Weintraub is a light-switch plate. Its whimsical snake mimics an Indian sand painting.*

Above: *To make these sumptuous shrine pins, Maria C. Moya uses an array of exquisite bits. Some of her pins carry the message "Wear Art"; others say, "Art Saves Lives."*

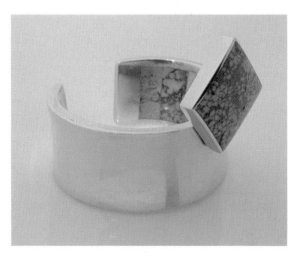

Right: *The solid weight of this generously proportioned gold cuff is given a slightly asymmetrical balance by its composition. But this bracelet by Allan Edgar and Judith Young also has a secret: A piece of turquoise for good luck is set inside the bracelet.*

Left: *Gail Bird, a Laguna/Santo Domingo Pueblo Indian, and Yazzie Johnson, a Navajo, worked together to create this prizewinning concho belt in sterling silver and 14K gold. The artists make only one or two of these belts each year.*

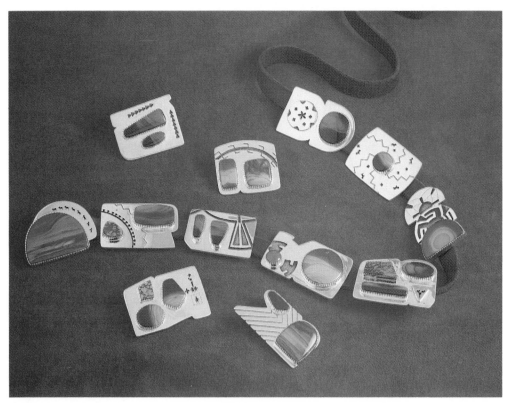

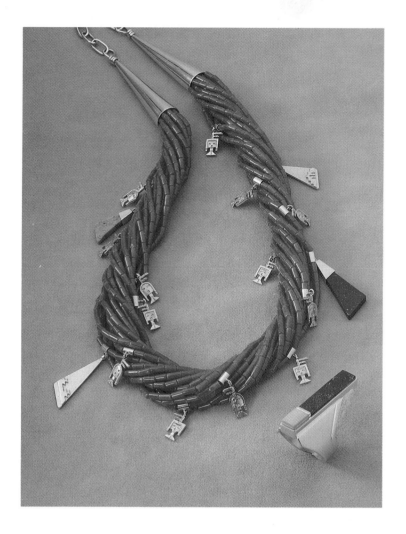

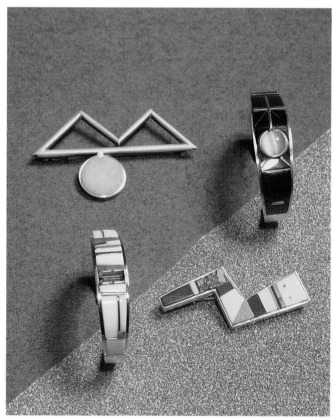

Above: James Little works with traditional stones, such as turquoise, lapis, and coral, but he introduces gold and geometric form to make a contemporary statement based on traditional Navajo motifs and design elements.

Right: The jewelry of Luis Mojica incorporates fine stones and a flawless finish to produce a futuristic look that simultaneously harks back to a primeval world of mountains and lightning bolts.

Above: Patricia Brady and Richard Weintraub work together to produce jewelry that combines several metalworking techniques and is set with precious stones. This landscape necklace, framed in silver cacti, depicts a gila monster slithering past a trio of coyotes howling at a pearl moon.

KACHINA DOLLS

The Pueblos' rich spiritual and ceremonial traditions are reflected and personified by the kachinas. Each kachina has three aspects: It is a supernatural being that has particular powers; it is a ritual dancer wearing a mask, body paint, and a costume that make him appear to be a deity, which is half human and half bird, animal, plant, or cloud; and it is a wooden doll given to little girls and babies. Kachina dolls introduce the child to the power of the kachinas and teach her the appropriate costume for each ritual dancer.

Before a kachina ceremony, a child's father or uncle makes her a doll that represents one of the kachinas that will take part in the dance. He starts with a cottonwood root, which he then shapes with a rasp and a penknife. Noses, horns, ears, and headdresses are whittled separately and attached to the dolls with small dowels. The kachina doll is given a smooth finish with a piece of sandstone and coated with kaolin. Colors are applied over the white undercoat, and feathers, yarn, or cloth are attached to complete the doll. Kachina dolls that are made for babies are much simpler than the ones made for girls. A baby's doll is cut out of a piece of board, which usually is not carved, and then crudely painted. Some recently made kachina dolls appear to be dancing. These dolls are often exquisitely carved and beautifully painted, but they are not traditional kachina dolls and are made to be sold to collectors.

The color and shape of a kachina's mask are symbolic, but masks made in different pueblos at different times may not represent the same kachina in exactly the same way. A mask's color indicates the direction from which the kachina comes to the dance, and symbols are often painted on the cheeks or forehead of the mask to identify it. The repertoire of symbols includes animal tracks, clouds, lightning, sun, moon, stars, corn, flowers, and geometric figures that convey particular meanings. These symbols are a clue to the identity of the kachina. Most kachina masks also have noses, mouths, and headdresses, which convey additional symbolic meaning.

Hopi and Zuni kachina dolls are an important element of Santa Fe design. Old kachina dolls, especially those made for babies, are the most valuable. Because kaolin does not bind with wood, the undercoat of old kachina dolls has often peeled away. The best nontraditional kachinas are incredibly detailed and beautifully carved and painted. In addition to making kachina dolls, some Pueblo woodcarvers, as well as jewelers and sculptors, use kachina masks and costumes in their work. Popular legend claims that kachina dolls are blessed with a spirit that comes out at night to wander about the house. In Santa Fe nothing having to do with spirit is easily dismissed, so this legend makes it seem especially desirable to have a kachina or a collection of kachinas on your mantel or coffee table.

Right: These Hopi kachina dolls are representations of the spiritual beings that are central to Pueblo religion. This collection includes Eagle, Ogre, Sun Face, and Crow Mother kachinas.

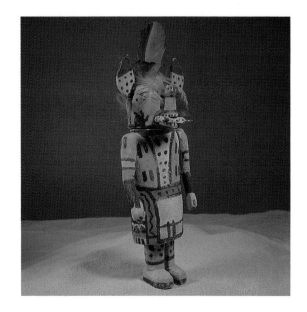

Left: *Tewaquaptewa, a Hopi kachina carver, used to dress up every day and sit in front of a house in Old Oraibi, the most ancient village on the Hopi mesas. He would converse with tourists while he worked, which caused some interesting and not always intentional evolutions in style and technique. This is one of his Coyote kachinas.*

Right: *Hopi kachinas live in the mountain range known as the San Francisco Peaks. Shown in front of these peaks are Crow Mother (Angwusnasomtaka) and We-u-u, who is part of the Bean Dance ceremony on Second Mesa. Crow Mother is one of the most important kachinas and presides over initiation ceremonies.*

Below left: *Pablik Mana, the Butterfly Maiden kachina, has become very glamorous and naturalistic in recent times, but in the early 1900s she was rendered in a much more abstract, fetishlike manner.*

Below right: *This beautiful group of Butterfly Maiden kachinas from the Heard Museum in Phoenix, Arizona, shows the evolution of form in kachina carving. The older examples from the early 1900s are on the right. They are simpler and less detailed; their clothing is described rather than delineated.*

Above: The Hemis kachinas, or Home Dancers, appear at the last few dances of the season, before the kachina spirits go home to the mountains. These old kachina dolls were carved by elders for children, who were told that the dolls came directly from the kachinas themselves.

Above right: This old kachina doll represents Ahöla. During the Bean Dance, a dancer portraying this kachina goes with the Powamu Chief to all the kivas and houses with ceremonial associations. They distribute the chief's bean and corn plants, and mark the doorways with four stripes of cornmeal in an appeal to the Cloud Chiefs to sit over these places.

Above: Early kachina dolls were carved with large feet so they could stand alone without being fastened to a base for display. This Hopi Malo kachina, distinguished by the stripe on its mask and other traditional details, was carved in the early 1900s.

Above: This Hemis kachina was carved by Nieto Lomahatewa in 1950. Since these dolls were used to teach children, their design elements are codified. But this carver chose to depart from tradition, giving the sash white markings instead of the conventional black ones and making a few other slight changes.

Left: *These contemporary Hopi wood sculptures draw their subject matter and some of their details from kachina dolls, but they are essentially decorative. This group of figures is by Wilmer and Wilfred Kaye.*

Above: *Contemporary Hopi kachinas are made to look as natural as possible. A kachina doll's kilt that would have been suggested with paint and carved as a simple cone now mimics a real dance costume. This Long Hair kachina, or Anak'china, was created by Ros George.*

Right: *Dennis Tewa, a contemporary Hopi kachina carver, achieves lifelike detail, especially in the hands and the separate quills on the feathers in this figure of a Deer kachina.*

Below left: *Kachina spirits play many roles in Hopi ceremonial life. The Prickly Pear Cactus Mana, Yunga Mana, is a joker figure. She pretends to give children piki (blue corn bread), but when they come to take it, she switches quickly and gives them prickly pear cactus. This figure was carved by Ronald Honyouti.*

Below: *This metal sculpture by Charles Pratt represents the kachina mask worn by a Talavai (Morning) kachina dancer.*

214

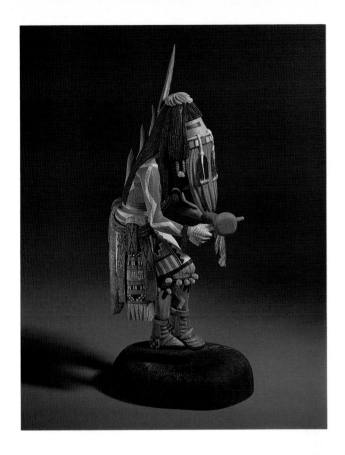

Above: *This highly complex, naturalistic dancer is a red-bearded Long Hair kachina created by Loren Phillips.*

Above right: *Hopi carver Cecil Calnimptewa made this Sun kachina and a companion Tühavi (the name means* paralyzed*). According to legend, the blind Sun kachina carried the paralyzed kachina on his back. Tühavi directed their course, and together they hunted and made their way on a long journey. When they reached their destination, the other kachinas cured them.*

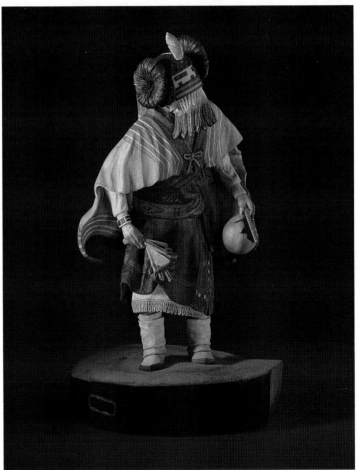

Above: *This beautifully carved, lifelike kachina figure by Dennis Tewa is a Kachin Mana. Her hair is painstakingly arranged in whorls on each side of her head, indicating that she is an unmarried maiden. After a Hopi woman marries, she traditionally wears her hair pulled back behind her ears.*

FURNITURE

Furniture making in New Mexico has a unique history that distinguishes it from other furniture-making traditions in the United States. Until the arrival of the Spanish colonist, there was essentially no wooden furniture in New Mexico. The Pueblos sat and slept on the floor. But the same *carpinteros* who constructed doors and corbels for the mission churches also used their woodworking tools to build simple furniture for the Spanish colonists. There are only a few remaining examples of the work of these early Spanish woodworkers, because furniture was destroyed along with everything else the Spanish colonists had built during the Pueblo uprising in the late seventeenth century. But histories of expeditions to Nuevo México and colonists' diaries contain detailed descriptions of the furniture built in the colony. These records along with collections of eighteenth and nineteenth century antiques give today's craftspeople the historical background they need to make accurate reproductions and contemporary furniture based on Spanish colonial designs.

During the late nineteenth century, most New Mexicans got rid of as much Spanish colonial furniture as they could. Like people in other parts of the country, they wanted to keep up with the latest styles from Europe. Local craftsmen and importers did their best to accommodate them, and there are many old photographs of rooms, even in adobe houses, filled with overstuffed chairs and other Victorian pieces. By 1920 Santa Fe furniture had returned to its Spanish heritage, but pieces built during the so-called Pueblo revival were larger and more comfortable than their historic counterparts.

The Taos bed is a good example of the way in which New Mexican furniture makers combined the solid comfort of mission furniture with Spanish colonial design elements. A Taos bed has a crosspiece that is similar to the back of a sofa linking the headboard and footboard, which are the same height. Some Taos beds are deep enough to accommodate a twin mattress, so they can be used as a guest bed. With the addition of bolsters and lots of pillows, a Taos bed becomes a comfortable couch that is roomy enough for serious relaxing.

Today's furniture makers create furniture that looks at home in both traditional and modern adobe interiors. Many of these pieces are clean, contemporary interpretations of classic furniture designs. But some are wildly colored and echo witty folk-art themes with carvings and bright decorations. There are many independent furniture makers and small cooperatives, as well as large New Mexico-based companies producing the kind of furniture used in Santa Fe design.

Right: David Cunningham calls this cabinet "Native American Bandstand." The painted trastero *is an entertaining mix of ideas and motifs that includes a dancer in high-top tennis shoes, a display of feathers, and a televised image of Dick Clark.*

Left: *This butterfly cradle is a collaboration by painter Hillary Riggs and cabinetmaker Peter Gould. It is made to stand alone or to hang from a beam in the ceiling in true Santa Fe style.*

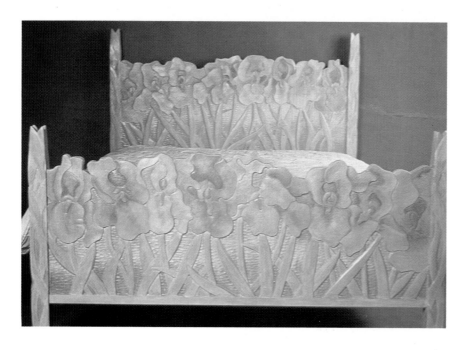

Left: *This dreamy bed wreathed in irises was designed by painter Hillary Riggs and carved by Peter Gould. Riggs then applied the color using a special process that allows the woodgrain to show through. The bed is part of the Sombraje Collection.*

Right: *Sombraje, headquartered in Dixon, New Mexico, originated furniture made with dyed branches. This Pueblo sofa and armchair are fine examples of the Sombraje Collection. The fabric and wall collage were designed by Sara McCook.*

■ *Above:* These willow shutters made by Sombraje are a staple of Santa Fe design. Their natural beauty enhances any room, and they also filter light without shutting it out completely. The chairs and table are from the Sombraje Collection.

■ *Above right:* This cheerful prickly pear coffee table by Bill Teetzel is a contemporary folk art masterpiece. Carved of pine in the shape of a locally common cactus, it is painted and stained to echo the real plant. The red fruit has burst into three blooms of stained glass, which are fashioned to hold votive candles.

■ *Above:* This stunning bed frame was actually made of old barn siding from a local landmark. But Peter Gould and Hillary Riggs enhanced the design with elements reminiscent of Navajo textiles, and this limited-edition piece from the Sombraje Collection became much more than a nostalgic recycling project.

219

Left: *New Mexican furniture with square lines, roomy proportions, and natural finishes is often described as Taos furniture because the style originated in Taos early in this century. This kind of furniture, like the pieces in this bedroom, is still available at a showroom appropriately called Taos Furniture.*

Below: *This secretary became a purely New Mexican piece when its designer, Bill Teetzel, gave it copper and brass door panels and put bullet details on the legs. Teetzel also crafted the sprightly little agave side table next to the secretary. The bloom is a lamp that has electric light bulbs set in stained glass.*

Above: *While visiting Santo Domingo Pueblo, architect Edmund A. Boniface was struck by the stepped formation of the headdress worn by a Butterfly Maiden kachina dancer. He designed this pristine maple chair with ebony inlay to reflect the image of the headdress.*

Above: *The softly weathered finishes on the furniture in the Sombraje Collection echo the patina on old Spanish pieces, which originally were brightly painted but have now worn to more subtle shades.*

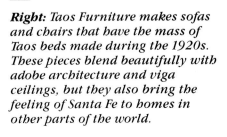

Above: Essential design elements in traditional New Mexico cabinets include door panels pierced to allow for ventilation. These pierced doors were cut with a holesaw and jigsaw; they are as beautiful as they are functional.

Above: An artistic association of craftspeople living near Dixon, New Mexico, eventually led to a shared exhibit space under the auspices of Sombraje, the originators of the willow furniture shown here. Colorist Hillary Riggs was instrumental in designing this room that brings together the work of potter Nausika Richardson, painter Walter Green, and carver David Parsons.

Right: Taos Furniture makes sofas and chairs that have the mass of Taos beds made during the 1920s. These pieces blend beautifully with adobe architecture and viga ceilings, but they also bring the feeling of Santa Fe to homes in other parts of the world.

Above: *This carved chest dates from the late eighteenth century. It was made in New Mexico, but it clearly shows the European heritage of the Spanish settlers in its graceful and intricate surface treatment of rampant lions, medallions, scallops, whorls, and rosettes.*

Above left: *This colonial chest from the collection of the Museum of International Folk Art is painted in an unusual manner. The design may have been influenced by Native American artifacts, such as the painted saddlebags made by Plains Indians.*

Left: *This massive nineteenth-century* trastero *was once painted green and brown, but the paint has worn down with age so that the woodgrain shows through. The top panels have jigsawed cutouts that may have been copied from pie safes brought in from Missouri.*

Right: This lovely chest incorporates rosettes, scallops, and nature motifs just as some of the early New Mexico colonial pieces did. But it was made recently by Peter Gould, and its colors and proportions are distinctly contemporary.

Left: This cowboy trastero by L.D. Burke III is exquisitely crafted, with fine detailing and subtly applied color. But real spurs and cattle horns won't allow this artful cabinet to take itself too seriously.

Left: Hispanic woodcarvers and cabinetmakers freely adapt their ancestors' designs to create a robust style that suits today's needs. This carved desk with its classic Spanish colonial design was made by Chris Sandoval for an office at Pecos National Monument, east of Santa Fe.

Left: Spanish colonists brought only a few treasured possessions with them when they came to live in Nuevo México. What they had they transported and stored in chests, or cajas, *like this one.*

223

Right: *Jim Wagner's painted furniture has its own astringent humor. In this cabinet he takes the clichéd motif of coyotes and pueblos to artful excess.*

Above: *Some of the most beautifully designed Santa Fe furniture is made by independent cabinetmakers who take pride in the solid structure and honest elegance of their work. Jim Dell's contemporary* trastero *is quietly opulent while remaining true to the natural aesthetic of New Mexico.*

Left: *This large* trastero *was crafted by Peter Gould, who used barn wood from a beloved Santa Fe landmark that finally had to come down. But this piece is set apart from other rough-hewn furniture by the tin bands that are inlaid in the panels. They are a direct reference to pierced-tin pie-safe doors, but Gould gives them a strikingly modern character.*

Below: *This cowboy* trastero *is the rugged, irreverent invention of L.D. Burke III, a cabinetmaker with his own unique view of Santa Fe design. There's a crown of real spurs on the pediment of this corner cabinet.*

Above: *L.D. Burke III created this hat rack of cattle horns mounted on a rough-hewn shelf that is reminiscent of colonial furniture made from adzed lumber. This piece is at once functional and humorous, a kind of parody of the American West, which has itself become almost a parody.*

Right: *A hugely enjoyable trend toward regional painted furniture with a folk twist was begun several years ago by Jim Wagner, whose small cabinet is shown here. It joins the image of a nursery-rhyme cow jumping over the moon with a quintessential New Mexican pickup truck.*

SCULPTURE

Sculpture as art, as opposed to sculpture as useful object or religious icon, is new to Santa Fe design. It has only come into its own during the last quarter century. But the sculpture now being made in Santa Fe covers a wide range of styles, from Indian sculpture of the Allan Houser school to traditional works, to abstract pieces and frankly wild nontraditional works.

Many abstract sculptors are influenced by the scale of the landscape around Santa Fe. The physical link between the human body and the slope and space of the terrain are interpreted in ways that range from mathematic to expressionistic. Other sculptors explore an element of the rich multicultural mix of people in Santa Fe. But some sculptors turn their backs on the landscape and the people, and focus instead on a single telling idea or scrap of information. In a singularly powerful way, the concentrated sculptures by these artists evoke a feeling of what it is like to move through Santa Fe's physical environment in three dimensions and perhaps the fourth dimension of time as well.

Right: The flowing composition of this piece sets up a harmony of parallel lines that evokes the special emotion between mother and child. Tim Nicola, a Native American sculptor of Penobscot descent, combines ageless themes with brilliant craftsmanship in this alabaster sculpture.

Above: R.C. Gorman is best known as a painter and graphic artist, but here he uses bronze to depict a solitary Indian woman. The sculpture echoes the theme of many of Gorman's lithographs.

Above: *Charles Pratt is a Native American artist of Cheyenne-Arapaho descent. This sculpture, "Two Feathers," is made of alabaster and brass.*

Above right: *Doug Hyde is a Native American artist of Nez Perce, Chippewa, and Assiniboin descent. In this piece he combines the image of a monumental Indian woman with an overstuffed chair to create a work that has universal meaning— the "Reluctant Babysitter."*

Left: *Doug Hyde is one of the most distinguished proteges of Allan Houser, the artist who almost single-handedly brought Native American art into the mainstream of American culture. In this work Hyde uses beautifully modeled bronze to depict the mysterious and commanding presence of an Indian woman.*

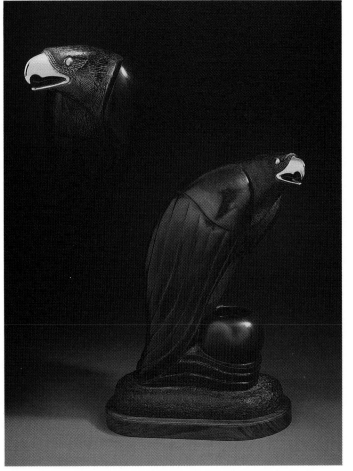

Above: *Chippewa-Cree sculptor Rollie Grandbois was one of the sculptors influenced by Allan Houser at the Institute of American Indian Arts. "Guardian of the Ancestors" is made of highly polished and darkly patinated bronze.*

227

Below: Carol Sarkisian celebrates the Southwest with a heavily beaded pair of leather cowboy boots she calls "Maurice's Boots."

Above: Sculptor Bob Haozous, who is a Native American of Apache descent, creates playful intersections of Indian and mainstream culture. His medium in this work entitled "Portable Pueblo" is steel plate.

Right: Santa Fe artist Stuart Ashman interprets a thunderbird in wood, metal, and bamboo. This wall-hung sculpture is 54 inches tall and looks toward the past as well as the future in its exuberant expression.

Below: John Connell's bronze raven is a rough, humble presence that is a reminder of the immediate experience of the essential Santa Fe.

Right: *Jan Beauboeuf graphically depicts Santa Fe life in this piece entitled "Wings of Love." The weathered wood contrasts perfectly with bright tubes of neon to create a vivid interplay between the old and the modern.*

Below right: *This "stone" piece by Art Brock seems to portray the rough geology of Santa Fe, yet surprisingly, it is made of glass, setting up an interesting interplay of opaqueness and transparency.*

Above: *Pedro Romero is a Hispanic sculptor whose work often deals with the concerns of the Hispanic population of Santa Fe. This ceramic piece, "Tierra y Libertad," is a poetic interpretation of a land-grant dispute.*

Left: *Ed Haddaway calls his painted steel sculpture "Apple Pickers' Song." The sprightly, dynamic piece is 11 feet tall.*

Above: *This rusty steel bird by Charles Southard soars high above the desert, seemingly free of the elegant pedestal that supports it. A bronze burro by Southard is permanently ensconced on a corner in downtown Santa Fe.*

Above: *The grassy sculpture gallery at Shidoni Foundry displays works fabricated and cast on the premises. In addition to the contemporary work shown here, the foundry also produces more traditional pieces.*

230

Above: *Shidoni Foundry and Gallery is one of the largest sculpture galleries in the United States. It was started in the late 1970s by Tommy Hicks, who continues to oversee every detail of production. The foundry is open to the public on Saturdays.*

Above right: *This elegant granite fountain by Jesús Bautista Moroles graces the interior patio of the Museum of Fine Arts. The work is about nine feet tall and evokes the grandeur of the mountains around Santa Fe.*

Above: *Luis Jimenez revisits a familiar Southwestern image in his fiberglass sculpture, "End of Trail." This eight-foot-tall, brilliantly colored piece is illuminated with working light bulbs.*

SANTOS

Handcrafted religious art in New Mexico is a vital art form, with modern masters, including Horacio Valdez, Luis Tapia, and Charles Carrillo, continuing a tradition that thrived in the eighteenth century. Like Pueblo kachina dolls, *santos* are not merely painted wooden figurines. They are objects of veneration and prayer that are created to bless the home. In traditional Hispanic households, *santos* have a special place of honor or stand on the family's altar.

Antique *santos* are exceedingly rare and highly collectible. But recently made statues also make a strong visual impact in a room that contains other folk art elements or Spanish colonial furniture. Both traditional and contemporary images of death are also found on mantels and shelves in Santa Fe homes. These ghastly skeletons were originally intended to remind the faithful that death was always at hand, but people who collect these figures today seem to concentrate on their primitive anatomy and the grim humor of their facial expressions.

Right: These bultos *(carved figurines) were made by José Benito Ortega around 1880. The* santero *lived in Mora, New Mexico, and worked with lumber sawed in a mill, which accounts for the flat appearance of the figures.*

Above: *Santoniño de Atocha was made by Charles Carrillo, who is considered to be the most* authentic *santero working today. Carrillo uses natural pigments, pine-sap varnish, cottonwood root, and historically correct details. For this* santo *he made a leather hat and a Taos-style pine chair, and painted a glazed-tile floor.*

Above: *This* retablo *(painted plaque) of San José was made by José Rafael Aragón. This nineteenth century artist depicted the saint with his symbol, a flowering staff, so that he is easily identifiable.*

Below: *Santa Barbara was carved by Horacio Valdez, a* santero *living in Dixon, New Mexico. Valdez is a self-taught craftsman whose work is displayed in many churches and chapels.*

Above: *This* nacimiento *(creche) is made of glazed and fired clay with natural pigments in the style of the Pueblo potters. Because of their subject matter, Indian-made* nacimientos *are considered to be* santos *even though they are not Spanish in style or origin.*

Above: *Santiago Matamoros (Saint James the Greater) is depicted on horseback. The anonymous carver, probably a follower of the Santoniño Santero, carved him wearing a colonial military uniform rather than the robes of biblical times.*

Above: *María Romero Cash gave her Nuestra Señora Soledad a bright tin crown. The artist is an important* santera, *whose family are well known in Santa Fe for their exquisite tinwork.*

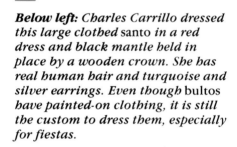

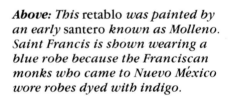

Below left: *Charles Carrillo dressed this large clothed* santo *in a red dress and black mantle held in place by a wooden crown. She has real human hair and turquoise and silver earrings. Even though* bultos *have painted-on clothing, it is still the custom to dress them, especially for fiestas.*

Above: *This* retablo *was painted by an early* santero *known as Molleno. Saint Francis is shown wearing a blue robe because the Franciscan monks who came to Nuevo México wore robes dyed with indigo.*

Above: *This* santo *was made by the Santoniño Santero in the 1850s and depicts Our Lady of the Rosary. The figure is made of cottonwood and has a cloth hoop skirt stiffened with gesso, which was painted to resemble lace.*

Below right: *The archangel San Rafaél is recognizable by the trout he is carrying. This* santo *was carved and painted by the Santoniño Santero during the mid-nineteenth century.*

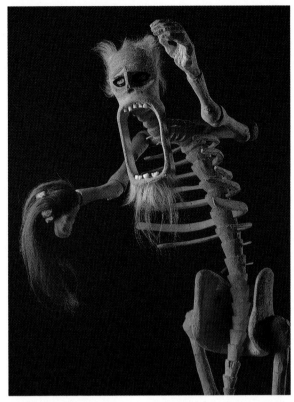

Above left: *This* bulto *and* retablo *were made by Charles Carrillo. The figure is Saint Joseph; the hand-adzed pine panel depicts the Virgin of Guadalupe. Carrillo is able to achieve deep but muted colors by using only natural pigments.*

Above right: *Doña Sebastiana is depicted by Luis Tapia in an unusual open-mouthed pose with a beard. Traditional* santos *show Death as a female figure with sunken eye sockets and a jagged sneer.*

Above: *San Acacio was a first-century martyr who was crucified by his enemies before he could convert to Christianity. José Rafael Aragón depicted the saint in colonial military clothing, which was the custom at the time.*

Above: *Santera María Romero Cash has added an elaborate tinwork crown embellished with golden disks to this dramatic* santo.

PAINTINGS AND PRINTS

The first painters to arrive in New Mexico from the East Coast settled not in Santa Fe but in Taos. Bert Phillips and Ernest Blumenschein, who had met while studying art in Paris, decided to stay on and paint in Taos when their wagon broke down there in the summer of 1898. But these men were only the vanguard of an impressive troop of skilled painters who have lived and worked in New Mexico. Mabel Dodge Luhan, a famed hostess, was responsible for encouraging many New York and European artists to come here. John Sloan, Randall Davey, B.J.O. Nordfeldt, E. Irving Couse, William Penhallow Henderson, and Andrew Dasburg all worked for a time in Santa Fe. George Bellows and Marsden Hartley summered here. In addition to Los Cincos Pintores (Fremont Ellis, Will Shuster, Jozef Bakos, Willard Nash, and Walter Mruk), the Santa Fe art colony included at one time or another such diverse talents as Alfred Morang, Theodore van Soelen, Victor Higgins, and Gustave Baumann.

Georgia O'Keeffe first visited Santa Fe in 1917. After returning for many summers, she settled in Abiquiu, a tiny village northwest of the city, in 1949. This area, including Ghost Ranch and the red cliffs of the Chama River Valley, became the subject matter for her most famous paintings.

Artists today still find as much variety and inspiration in the New Mexico landscape as the early painters did, but painters working today are more free to interpret what they see. There is no single Santa Fe painting style. But there is one element that ties Santa Fe art together: It is art about what it is like to be here. Paintings made here range from personal variations on contemporary art forms to the exuberantly colorful to the seriously wild, but the best artists continue to look unflinchingly at the human experience and then conceive forms with which to present their ideas.

Several elements work on an artist's vision here: the history, the land, the light, and the camaraderie of the arts colony. The scale of the landscape influences even abstract painters. The clear air unmasks the heavy color saturation of both the terrain and the human presence. The altitude and the ultraviolet rays, as well as sudden temperature changes, thunder showers, and snowstorms, show up in the texture of many painters' canvases. The extended arts community acts as a catalyst for an artist's ideas. No one in Santa Fe has to work in isolation.

Both large and small Santa Fe art galleries show and promote local artists. Santa Fe now has nearly 200 art galleries, not all of which concentrate exclusively on work produced locally. Some people have worried that the distinctive qualities of Santa Fe painting may be lost, but there is no need to worry. Santa Fe painters can depend on their history and the immaculate desert light to keep them clear-eyed as they accept new influences. Artists here have always had a robust vigor that embraces and refines the inevitably changing world that is the legacy of every artist, everywhere.

Right: In *"Through the Greasewood"* (oil, 45 by 43 inches), Santa Fe painter E. Martin Hennings (1886–1956) positioned riders on horseback in a visually powerful composition of sloping planes and chamisa.

Left: Georgia O'Keeffe (1887–1986) lived in the village of Abiquiu, north of Santa Fe, for forty years. She made the landscape her own, creating a reality through her work that is stripped of unnecessary clutter and meaningless imagery. This 1936 painting is entitled "Red Hills and Pedernal" (oil on canvas, 20 by 30 inches).

Below: This painting, "Road Past the View II" (oil on canvas, 24 by 30 inches), shows the way in which Georgia O'Keeffe abstracted forms without robbing them of their intrinsic meaning.

R.C. Gorman □ Indian Market 1985 □ Enthios Gallery □ Santa Fe

Above: Posters and lithographs by R.C. Gorman are sold in galleries in many parts of the United States. This image of a finely drawn Indian woman, which is a poster for Indian Market 1985, is typical of Gorman's work.

Right: New Mexico modernists were a loosely affiliated group of painters who sought to interpret their environment in pared-down, abstract terms. Andrew Dasburg was one the most influential of these painters. "My Gate on the Camino" (oil on canvas, 13 by 16 inches) is one of his New Mexico paintings.

238

Above: *Alfred Morang (1901–1958) painted landscapes in an impressionistic style. This painting, "Camino sin Nombre" (oil on board, 18 by 22 inches), was made in about 1940.*

Above: *Jozef Bakos (1891–1977) was one of Los Cincos Pintores, a group of five painters who founded Santa Fe's arts colony. His 1923 painting "The Springtime Rainbow" (oil, 29½ by 35½ inches) is one of the most popular paintings at the Museum of Fine Arts.*

Right: *B.J.O. Nordfeldt (1878–1955) lived in Santa Fe during the 1920s and 1930s. This landscape, "Three White Horses" (oil, 16 by 22 inches), is typical of the painter's New Mexico work and is rendered with direct and vigorous brushwork.*

Right: *William Penhallow Henderson (1877–1943) created murals, illustrations, handcrafted furniture, stage designs, and innovative architectural projects in addition to paintings and pastels. This painting made around 1917 is "Paintbrush, Roses and Yucca" (oil on board, 16 by 20 inches).*

Left: E. Irving Couse (1866–1936) began coming to New Mexico in 1903; he settled permanently in Taos in 1927. His paintings of Indians, such as "La Chucunga" (oil on board, 20 by 16 inches), were used to illustrate the widely distributed calendars issued by the Atchison, Topeka and Santa Fe Railway Company.

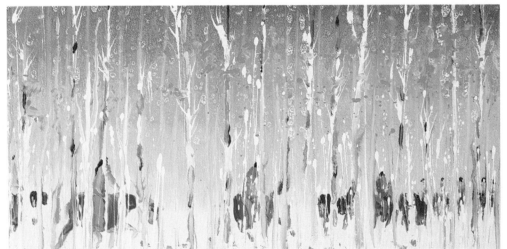

Left: Earl Biss, a Crow Indian who studied at the Institute of American Indian Arts with Fritz Scholder and Allan Houser, is known for the radiant, painterly quality of his canvases, such as this one, "Late in the Moon of the Falling Leaves" (oil, 10 by 20 inches).

Right: John Sloan (1871–1951) was a mentor of Santa Fe art. He advised the directors of the art museum, encouraged younger artists, and helped create an audience for Santa Fe art in New York, where he taught at the Art Students League. Sloan established a home in Santa Fe in 1920 and returned every summer to paint. This painting, "Squaws in the Dance" (oil, 20 by 24 inches), is one of his New Mexico images.

Above: *Theodore van Soelen (1890–1964) came to New Mexico for his health in 1916. His insightful portraits of the people and the land are rendered with a highly polished technique. In this painting, "Shadows" (oil on canvas, 36 by 40 inches), he controlled the sentimentality of the narrative situation by calling attention to the shadow of a lone tree that is outside the picture plane.*

Above: *Joseph Henry Sharp (1859–1953) devoted his life to recording the rapidly vanishing traditional way of life of the Plains, Navajo, and Pueblo peoples. "Hunting Son" (oil, 24 by 20 inches) is one of his paintings of a Plains Indian.*

Right: *Randall Davey, who taught at the University of New Mexico in Albuquerque, maintained a studio on Upper Canyon Road in Santa Fe. Davey is best known for his portraits and horse racing scenes, but "Market Day" (oil on board, 30 by 23 inches) is a spirited look at everyday life in a Mexican village.*

241

242

Left: This landscape, "Late Afternoon Storm" (29½ by 41 inches), by printmaker Eric Lindgren is a monotype. It was made by a one-time-only printmaking process in which the plate is not etched but has paint applied to it directly. Lindgren frequently makes several plates for each monotype, achieving rich and subtle results.

Right: The vastness of the New Mexico landscape is captured in this long, horizontal composition by Joan Foth. The elegantly rendered watercolor, "Sangre de Cristos" (28 by 72 inches), depicts a mountain range near Santa Fe.

Right: "Embudo Orchard" (oil, 30 by 22 inches) by Robert Daughters portrays the natural beauty and somber magic of the farmland along the Rio Grande.

Left: The adobe images of painter Roger Sprague radiate an incredible quality of reflected light. He achieves this with brilliantly colored underpainting, which he then works up to a cool, serene finish that nevertheless glows with hidden depths. This painting, "Church at Laguna" (48 by 60 inches), is oil on linen.

Right: Richard Maitland, a surrealist with decidedly personal imagery, has made the special magic and absurdity of New Mexico his subject for two decades. This poster, "Party in Santa Fe," is one of his gentle but telling comments on life.

Right: In this lithograph, "Ranchos de Taos" (30 by 39½ inches), Ron Robles creates a subtle architectural composition by casting his own understated light on one of the most often painted and photographed buildings in New Mexico.

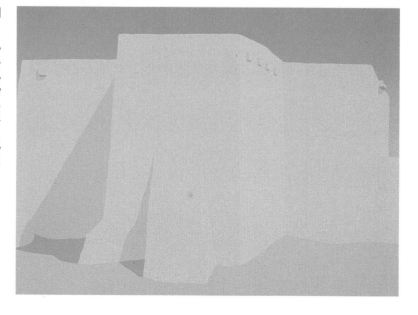

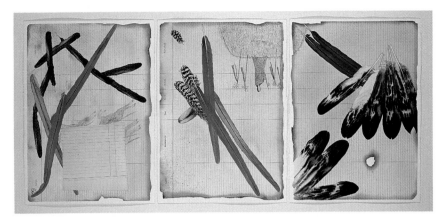

Above: The wide open spaces, the clear air, and crisp lines of the landscape contrast with a relentless human presence in this lithograph, "Interstate" (24 by 22 inches), by Woody Gwyn.

Above: In "El Sombrero" (oil and acrylic on photo linen, 48 by 108 inches), Bob Wade heats up a scene from the Wild West with a jolt of contemporary awareness.

Above right: This triptych from the ledger series by Al Lostetter makes a statement about the injustices of the western expansion of the United States without beating the viewer over the head with its message. Ledger paper, feathers, a burnt hole, and childlike drawings are brought together to create a sense of imbalance and loss. The work on paper is 22 by 45 inches.

Right: John Axton's painting, "Western Stars" (oil, 20 by 30 inches), depicts the subtle mystery of a Santa Fe evening by concealing more than it reveals.

Left: *Tavlos first included the howling coyote in his work years ago; now it shows up on everything from earrings to T-shirts. What began as a personal expression of anguish and defiant joy has become something of a Santa Fe cliché, but even though the image is well known, it hasn't lost its power. This painting is entitled "Felix Coshare Coyote Singing That Ol' Love Song 'All of Me' Hoping That Tonight's the Night He's Been Waiting For" (acrylic on fiberboard, 48 by 74 inches).*

Right: *Fran Larsen is a humorist whose paintings are so vibrant that she does not choose to restrain them within their frames. In this work, "Picture Post Cards from the Pueblo" (mixed media, 32 by 56 inches), a rainbow cum lightning bolt bounces off the top of a brightly embellished frame, while within her watercolor painting itself flamingo tourists enjoy sights of Santa Fe.*

Left: *Frank Howell can do it all. He's a painter, lithographer, poet, and writer, and he also runs several galleries. This print, "Plains Madonna" (9½ by 18 inches), is typical of his visual art in which he uses incredible detail to create a universal image.*

Above: "Nube Roja" (acrylic, 24 by 30 inches) by David Barbero presents syncopated, semiabstract landforms outlined in subtle colors.

Above: John Nieto chooses bright, vivid colors, not always associated with the desert and Santa Fe, to express the intense light and strong life force he finds here. This acrylic painting is entitled "Navaho Madonna" (60 by 48 inches).

Right: International artist Dan Namingha is a direct descendant of Hopi potter Nampeyo. In this painting of Kwahu (Eagle kachina), the artist uses bold compositions to interpret his background with contemporary exuberance. "Kwahu" (80 by 70 inches) is acrylic on canvas.

FOLK ART

Right: The folk artist who made this plaque uses the trade name Peacock Soup. Her whimsical wall pieces are cut from metal and brightly painted. In her work she creates a charming universe where nursery rhymes, Hopi mythology, desert mirage, and world folklore coexist in cheerful idiosyncracy.

The term *folk art* can refer to naive painting or to sculpture and other decorative elements that were made by someone who had no formal art training. But this broad definition includes everything from kachina dolls and *santos* to territorial furniture and the homemade Victorian gingerbread that was once added to some adobe houses. Much of the work made in the Southwest by highly skilled potters, weavers, woodcarvers, and other craftspeople during the course of many hundreds of years is in a sense folk art. But in Santa Fe today, it seems more appropriate to use the term *folk art* to describe intentionally unrefined decorative objects, such as Felipe Archuleta's animal sculptures, Paul Lutonsky's brightly colored snakes, and Alonzo Jiménez's howling coyotes. Brilliant color and good humor are often components of folk art made in Santa Fe or imported to Santa Fe from Mexico. These objects add a charming touch to rooms that otherwise might seem to take themselves too seriously.

Above: "Gallery Dog" by Billy Rodriguez is a sly poke at the gallery scene in Santa Fe. The artist, who is descended from early Spanish settlers, is the father of Chalo Rodriguez. Both men are known for the whimsical personalities of their carved creatures.

Above: *Folk artist Carolyn Peacock crafts these delightful wall decorations from tin. Most of her pieces are purely Santa Fe, but some recall toys and puppets from other parts of the world. Many of these painted ornaments have movable parts.*

Above right: *Chalo Rodriguez is a talented woodcarver. He is known for the surprising details with which he decorates his animals. This African civet has real marbles for its spooky eyes.*

Above: *La Mesa (the table) is a Santa Fe store that specializes in bringing together pottery and folk art made by local craftspeople. In this artful mingling of color, texture, and form, high-fired dinnerware is displayed with a stipple-glazed hand-made pitcher and stylized saguaro cacti.*

Left: *Hector Rascon carved these winsome animals and their patron, Saint Francis, who is also the patron of Santa Fe. Rascon is a member of one of the Hispanic families who specialize in carving and painting local animals.*

Right: Chalo Rodriguez carves figures that are deliberately primitive, yet they exert the same hypnotic menace as gargoyles. The color composition of Rodriguez's work gives it a unique sophistication.

Above: Jil Gurule crafts these exquisite ceramic miniatures of the mission churches at the Indian pueblos and Spanish villages around Santa Fe.

Below: Christmas in Santa Fe fills the local shops with an array of ornaments unique to the Southwest. These charming miniatures are from the collection of The Shop on San Francisco Street, a year-round source for Christmas folk art.

Right: This lovely old Isleta-style frame was crafted from a lard tin. The label was never meant to show; it would have been covered by a family photograph or a religious picture. The Isleta style is characterized by narrow glass panels that are painted on the back with bold designs before they are fitted into the frame.

Left: These two Hispanic folk art animals were carved by David Alvarez.

Right: This touchingly ferocious jungle creature was carved by Billy Rodriguez. It is a big cat: 32 inches long and 21 inches high. Despite its sharp, pointed tin teeth and aggressive stance, its wistful eyes seem merely puzzled.

SANTA FE DESIGN RESOURCES

SANTA FE BY MAIL

Los Chileros de Nuevo Mexico
P.O. Box 6215
Santa Fe, New Mexico 87502
(505) 471-6967
Authentic food supplies and chile ristras

New Millenium Fine Arts
217 W. Water Street
Santa Fe, New Mexico 87501
(505) 983-2002
Inexpensive posters and art

Posters of Santa Fe, Inc.
111 E. Palace Avenue
Santa Fe, New Mexico 87501
(505) 982-6645
The best poster images

SPECIAL THINGS

Arius Tiles
114 Don Gaspar Avenue
Santa Fe, New Mexico 87501
(505) 983-5563
Art tiles and tile murals

Blue Raven Construction Works
2867 Cook Road
Santa Fe, New Mexico 87501
Mailing address:
P.O. Box 5468
Santa Fe, New Mexico 87502
(505) 471-6053
Designers, artists, and builders

Counter Point Tile
P.O. Box 2132
Santa Fe, New Mexico 87504
(505) 982-1247
Handmade tiles for fireplaces, bathrooms, and kitchens

David Samora Cabinet Maker
2873 All Trades Road
Santa Fe, New Mexico 87505
(505) 471-5728
Fine corbels, doors, and cabinets

Dell Woodworks
1326 Rufina Circle
Santa Fe, New Mexico 87505
(505) 471-3005
Santa Fe-style furniture

Design Center of Santa Fe
418 Cerrillos Road
Santa Fe, New Mexico 87501
(505) 983-3434
Design showroom

Origins
135 W. San Francisco Street
Santa Fe, New Mexico 87501
(505) 988-2323
Fine jewelry and clothing

Taos Furniture
1807 2nd Street
Santa Fe, New Mexico 87505
(505) 988-1229
Furniture for comfort

Tierra Wools
P.O. Box 118
Los Ojos, New Mexico 87551
(505) 588-7231
Wool growers and artisans

SANTA FE SHOPS

Artesanos Imports Co.
P.O. Drawer G
Santa Fe, New Mexico 87504
(505) 983-5563
Tiles and everything else from Mexico

Jackalope Pottery
2820 Cerrillos Road
Santa Fe, New Mexico 87501
(505) 471-8539
Imports appropriate for Santa Fe design

Kachina House & Gallery
236 Delgado
Santa Fe, New Mexico 87501
(505) 982-8415
Fine old collection

Packard's Indian Trading Co.
61 Old Santa Fe Trail
Santa Fe, New Mexico 87501
(505) 983-9241
Contemporary Indian crafts

Santa Fe Pottery
1425 Paseo de Peralta
Santa Fe, New Mexico 87501
(505) 988-7687
Dishes and tableware

The Shop
208 W. San Francisco Street
Santa Fe, New Mexico 87501
(505) 983-4823
Folk art, Christmas all year, and colonial antiques

SANTA FE ART GALLERIES

Altermann & Morris Galleries
225 Canyon Road #11
Santa Fe, New Mexico 87501
(505) 983-1590
19th and 20th Century American

Cline Fine Art Gallery
526 Canyon Road
Santa Fe, New Mexico 87501
(505) 986-0880
Classic art

The Contemporary Craftsman
130 Lincoln Avenue
Santa Fe, New Mexico 87501
(505) 988-1001
Longtime crafts gallery

Contemporary Southwest Galleries
123 W. Palace Avenue
Santa Fe, New Mexico 87501
(505) 986-0440
Bright, bold art

Cristof's
106 W. San Francisco Street
Santa Fe, New Mexico 87501
(505) 988-9881
Big selection of Navajo rugs

David Rettig Fine Arts
901 W. San Mateo
Santa Fe, New Mexico 87504
(505) 983-4640
Works by Bob Haozous

Dewey Galleries, Ltd.
74 E. San Francisco Street
Santa Fe, New Mexico 87501
(505) 982-8632
*Indian pots, rugs, and jewelry;
Western art; and antiques*

Economos
500 Canyon Road
Santa Fe, New Mexico 87501
(505) 982-6347
*Antique Indian art and Spanish
colonial furniture*

Elaine Horwitch Galleries
129 W. Palace Avenue
Santa Fe, New Mexico 87501
(505) 988-8997
Contemporary and well-known artists

Ernesto Mayans Galleries
601 Canyon Road
Santa Fe, New Mexico 87501
(505) 983-8068
Where the past meets the future

Fenn Galleries
1075 Paseo de Peralta
Santa Fe, New Mexico 87501
(505) 982-4631
*Early Santa Fe painters and Indian
artifacts*

The Frank Howell Gallery
103 Washington Avenue
Santa Fe, New Mexico 87501
(505) 984-1074 (800) 234-1074
Home base for the artist

Gerald Peters Gallery
P.O. Box 908
Santa Fe, New Mexico 87504
(505) 988-8961
*Contemporary and early
masterworks*

Glenn Green Galleries
50 E. San Francisco Street
Santa Fe, New Mexico 87501
(505) 988-4168
Paintings by Allan Houser

Graphics House
702 Canyon Road
Santa Fe, New Mexico 87501
(505) 983-2654
Excellent print collection

Hand Graphics Gallery
418 Montezuma Avenue
Santa Fe, New Mexico 87501
(505) 988-1241
Printmaking gallery and atelier

James Jereb Studio
1001 E. Alameda Street
Santa Fe, New Mexico 87501
(505) 989-8765
*Berber tribal textiles, jewelry, and folk
art*

Jamison Galleries
560 Montezuma Avenue, Suite 103
Santa Fe, New Mexico 87501
(505) 982-3666
High quality art

Joshua Baer & Company
116½ Palace Avenue
Santa Fe, New Mexico 87501
(505) 988-8944
Museum-quality Indian artifacts

Kania-Ferrin Gallery
662 Canyon Road
Santa Fe, New Mexico 87501
(505) 982-8767
Antique Indian baskets

Keats Gallery
644 Canyon Road
Santa Fe, New Mexico 87501
(505) 982-6686
Collages

La Mesa of Santa Fe
225 Canyon Road
Santa Fe, New Mexico 87501
(505) 984-1688
Tabletop gallery

LewAllen-Butler Fine Art
129 W. Palace Avenue
Santa Fe, New Mexico 87501
(505) 988-8997
Collectible art

Linda Durham Gallery
400 Canyon Road
Santa Fe, New Mexico 87501
(505) 988-1313
New Mexico experimental artists

Linda McAdoo Galleries, Ltd.
503 Canyon Road
Santa Fe, New Mexico 87501
(505) 983-7182 Fax: (505) 984-0152
Classic Taos style

Mariposa/Santa Fe
225 Canyon Road
Santa Fe, New Mexico 87501
(505) 982-3032
Top-quality crafts

Morning Star Gallery Ltd.
513 Canyon Road
Santa Fe, New Mexico 87501
(505) 982-8187
Antique tribal art

Munson Gallery
225 Canyon Road
Santa Fe, New Mexico 87501
(505) 983-1657
Dazzling landscape paintings

Nedra Matteucci Fine Art
1075 Paseo de Peralta
Santa Fe, New Mexico 87501
(505) 982-4631
Gracious traditional art

Owings-Dewey Fine Art
74 E. San Francisco Street
Santa Fe, New Mexico 87501
(505) 982-6244
Classic art

Peter Waidler Gallery
125 N. Guadalupe Street
Santa Fe, New Mexico 87501
(505) 989-3333
Wildly modern art

Shidoni Galleries
P.O. Box 250
Tesuque, New Mexico 87574
(505) 988-8001
Sculpture of the American West

The Sombraje Collection
544 Guadalupe Street
Santa Fe, New Mexico 87501
(505) 988-5567
Santa Fe design

Ventana Fine Art
211 Old Santa Fe Trail
Santa Fe, New Mexico 87501
(505) 983-8815
Paintings and sculpture

Wadle Galleries Ltd.
128 W. Palace Avenue
Santa Fe, New Mexico 87501
(505) 983-9219
Popular Santa Fe art

White Hyacinth, A Poster Gallery
137 W. San Francisco Street
Santa Fe, New Mexico 87501
(505) 983-2831
Distinctive collection

MUSEUMS

Guadalupe Historic Foundation
100 Guadalupe Street
Santa Fe, New Mexico 87501
(505) 988-2027

Institute of American Indian Arts Museum
1639 Cerrillos Road
Santa Fe, New Mexico 87501
(505) 988-6281

Museum of Fine Arts
107 W. Palace Avenue
Santa Fe, New Mexico 87504
(505) 829-4456

Museum of Indian Arts & Culture
710 Camino Lejo
Santa Fe, New Mexico 87504
(505) 827-8941

Museum of International Folk Art
706 Camino Lejo
Santa Fe, New Mexico 87504
(505) 827-8350

Museum of New Mexico Shops
(24-hour information):
(505) 827-6463

Palace of the Governors
Palace Avenue
Santa Fe, New Mexico 87504
(505) 827-6476

Wheelwright Museum of American Indian
704 Camino Lejo
Santa Fe, New Mexico 87502
(505) 982-4636

ARCHITECTS

Architects Santa Fe
466 W. San Francisco Street
Santa Fe, New Mexico 87501
(505) 983-5497

Bruce Davis Architect
Route 9, P.O. Box 90 B.D.
Santa Fe, New Mexico 87505
(505) 983-9178

Ellis/Browning Architects
560 Montezuma Avenue, Suite 202
Santa Fe, New Mexico 87501
(505) 984-2344

Van H. Gilbert Architect
319 Central N.W., Suite 201
Albuquerque, New Mexico 87102
(505) 247-9955

Kells and Craig Architects, Inc.
201 Coal S.W.
Albuquerque, New Mexico 87102
(505) 243-2724

Berry Langford Architect
1700 Lafayette N.E.
Albuquerque, New Mexico 87106
(505) 256-7879

Lloyd & Tryk Architects
301 N. Guadalupe Street, Suite 201
Santa Fe, New Mexico 87501
(505) 988-9789 (505) 982-8556

Mazria Associates, Inc.
607 Cerrillos Road, Suite G
Santa Fe, New Mexico 87504
(505) 988-5309

Pearson & Co. Architects
9401 Haines N.E.
Albuquerque, New Mexico 87112
(505) 293-6900

Robert W. Peters, A.I.A.
1 Loop One N.W.
Albuquerque, New Mexico 87120
(505) 899-0454

Jim Satzinger, Architects/Builders
1807 2nd Street, Suite 27
Santa Fe, New Mexico 87505
(505) 927-2938

Spears Architect, A.I.A.
1334 Pacheco Street
Santa Fe, New Mexico 87501
(505) 983-6966

Studio Arquitectura
322 Montezuma Avenue
Santa Fe, New Mexico 87501
(505) 982-5338

Westwork Architects
2403 San Mateo Boulevard N.E., Suite S2
Albuquerque, New Mexico 87110
(505) 884-5252

INTERIOR DESIGNERS

Charles David Interiors
205 Delgado
P.O. Box 5218
Santa Fe, New Mexico 87502
(505) 988-9629

Susan Dupepe Interior Design
112 W. San Francisco Street, Suite 314
Santa Fe, New Mexico 87501
(505) 982-4536

Pamela D. Earnest Interiors
5200 Eubank N.E., Suite E11
Albuquerque, New Mexico 87111
(505) 293-0880

Hayslip Design Associates
343 W. Manhattan Street
Santa Fe, New Mexico 87501
(505) 983-2147
2602 McKinney Avenue, Suite 400
Dallas, Texas 75204
(214) 871-9106

James Jereb Design
1001 E. Alameda Street
Santa Fe, New Mexico 87501
(505) 989-8765

Kailer-Grant Designs
143 Lincoln Avenue
Santa Fe, New Mexico 87501
(505) 983-6449

Patrician Design Interiors
216-A Gold Avenue S.W.
Albuquerque, New Mexico 87102
(505) 242-7646

Robert Strell
1301 Lopez Road S.W.
Albuquerque, New Mexico 87105
(505) 877-8311

INDEX

A
Abiquiu, 236
Acoma Pueblo 21, 188, 191
  potters, 180, 185, 193
Adams, Ansel, 41
Adobe, 16
  bricks, 26–27
  walls, 27, 32, 33, 97
Ahöla kachina, 213
Albuquerque, New Mexico, 31, 35–36, 38
  Old Town, 159
Alcobas, 130–41
Alvarez, David, 251
American Territory, 32–37
Anasazi, 10–15, 16, 19, 22, 43, 62, 98, 146, 174
Apaches, 24, 174
  baskets, 174, 175, 176, 177
Applegate, Frank, 42
Aragón, José Rafael, 29, 233, 235
Archuleta, Felipe, 248
Archuleta-Sagel, Theresa, 194
Ashman, Stuart, 228
Atchison, Topeka and Santa Fe Railway, 35
Atwill, Doug, 242
Axton, John, 245

B
Baca, José Albino, 34
Bakos, Jozef, 236, 239
Bancos, 27, 69, 79, 80–81, 91, 107, 130, 162, 165, 168
Baños, 142–47
Barbero, David, 247
Basket Makers, 10
Baskets, 174–79
  prehistoric, 10, 177
Bathrooms, 142–47
Baumann, Gustave, 236
Beauboeuf, Jan, 229
Becknell, William, 30
Bedrooms, 130–41
Begay, Harvey, 204
Bellows, George, 236
Bird, Gail, 208
Biss, Earl, 246
Blue Corn, 185
Blumenschein, Ernest, 236
Boniface, Edmund A., 220
Bosque Redondo, New Mexico, 194
Brady, Patricia, 208, 209
Brock, Art, 229
Bultos, 29, 232, 235
Burke, David, 140, 141
Burke III, L.D., 223, 225
Burnt Water textiles, 200
Butterfly Maiden kachina, 212, 220

C
Cajas. See Chests
Calnimptewa, Cecil, 215
Carpinteros, 28–29, 216
Carrillo, Charles, 232, 234, 235
Carter/Satzinger, 67, 76
Cash, Maria Romero, 233, 235
Cathedral of Saint Francis, 26, 31
Chaco Canyon National Monument, New Mexico, 14–15
Chaco masonry, 68, 148–49
Charles-David Interiors, 79
Chemehuevi baskets, 174, 177
Cherry/See Architects, 69, 111
Chests, 28, 74, 130, 223
Chihuahua, Mexico, 31
Chimayo, New Mexico, 27, 194
Chino, Grace, 188
Cliff dwellings, 12–13

Cliff Palace, 12–13
Cochiti Pueblo, 182
  pottery, 190
Cocinas, 108–21
Colcha embroidery, 194, 199, 203
Colorado Plateau, 10
Colorado River, 8
Comedores, 98–107
Connell, John, 228
Corbels, 27, 71, 88–89, 93, 156
Cordero, Helen, 190
Corn Maiden kachina, 186, 206
Coronado, Francisco Vasquez de, 24
Couse, E. Irving, 236, 240
Coyote kachina, 212
Crespin, Don Gregorio, 165
Crow Mother kachina, 178, 211–12
Cunningham, David, 216–17
Curtin, Leonora, 42

D
Da, Popovi, 184, 189, 192
Da, Tony, 180
Dasburg, Andrew, 41, 236, 238
Daughters, Robert, 243
Davey, Randall, 236, 241
Davis, Bruce, 68, 129
Deer kachina, 214
Dell, Jim, 224
Dens, 122–29
Denver and Rio Grande Railroad, 35
Depression, economic, 42
Deyuse, Leekya, 206
Dining rooms, 98–107
Doors, wooden, 27, 64, 68

E
Eagle kachina, 211
Edgar, Allan, 207, 208
Ellis, Fremont 236
  house, 89, 154
El Paso, 26
El Valle, 194
Entradas, 64–73
Entryways, 64–73
Equipale furniture, 86, 87, 165
Española, 24
Evans, Anne, 40

F
Fathy, Hasson, 60
Fenn, Forrest, 164–65
Fiesta de Santa Fe, 7
Fireplaces, 27, 74, 83–84, 88–89, 90–91, 105, 139, 146
Folk art, 248–51
Fort Leavenworth, Kansas, 32
Fort Stanton, New Mexico, 36
Fort Sumner, New Mexico, 36
Fort Union National Monument, New Mexico, 32–33, 64
Foth, Joan, 243
Four Corners area, 22, 194, 197
Franciscan Order of Friars, 24
Furniture, 28–29, 216–25

G
Ganado Red, 194
Garcia, Rose Chino, 188, 191
Gardens, 162–71
George, Ros, 214
Germantown yarn, 198, 199
Ghost Ranch, 236
Gilbert, Van, 81
Gilpin, Laura, 40, 41
Gonzáles, Barbara, 184
Gonzáles, Rose, 188
Gorman, R.C., 226, 238
Gould, Peter, 218, 219, 223, 224
Grandbois, Rollie, 227
Greek revival architecture, 32, 53
Green, Walter, 140–41, 221
Gurule, Jil, 250

Gutierrez de la Cruz, Lois, 185
Gwyn, Woody, 245

H
Haciendas, 31
  Spanish colonial, 54–55, 57
  territorial, 34–35
Haddaway, Ed, 230
Hall, Russel, 140–41
Haozous, Bob, 228
Hartley, Marsden, 41, 236
Hawley, Mike, 184
Hemis kachina, 213
Henderson, William Penhallow, 236, 239
Hennings, E. Martin, 236–37
Hicks, Tommy, 231
Higgins, Victor, 236
Hohokam, 10, 174
Holmes, Sabatini, and Eeds, 69, 96–97, 134–35
Home Dancers, 213
Honyouti, Ronald, 214
Hopi
  baskets, 174, 178–79
  kachina dolls, 210–15
  pottery, 180, 183, 184
  villages, 16
Hopper, Edward, 41
Hornos. See Fireplaces
Houser, Allan, 226, 227, 240
Howell, Frank, 246
Hyde, Doug, 226–27

I
Independence, Missouri, 30
Indian Market, 6, 197
Isleta, New Mexico, 19
  style, 251

J
Jackson, William Henry, 13
Jaramillo-Lavadie, Juanita, 194
Jardines, 162–71
Jereb, James, 64–65, 66–67, 122–23
Jewelry, 204–9
Jiménez, Alonzo, 248
Jimenez, Luis, 231
Johnson, Nestor, Mortier, and Rodriguez, 84, 134, 140, 151, 172–73
Johnson, Whitman, 242
Johnson, Yazzie, 208

K
Kachina dolls, 210–15
Kachinas, 4, 178, 179
Kailer-Grant Designs, 87, 120–21, 140
Ka-k'ok-shi (Good Dance), 20
Kaye, Wilmer and Wilfred, 214
Kearny, Steven Watts, 32
Kells and Craig Architects, 68, 83
Kenton, Beatrice, 176
Keoni, Victoria, 200–201
KiMo Theatre, 38–39, 40
Kitchens, 108–21
Kivas, 10, 14, 16, 48–49
Krieger, Heath, 193

L
La Cienega, New Mexico, 7, 27
La Fonda Hotel, 40
Laguna pottery, 180
La Luz Condominiums, 42–43, 44
Lamy, Juan Bautista, 31
Lamy, New Mexico, 35
Larsen, Fran, 246
Las Vegas, New Mexico, 34, 35–36, 142
Latillas, 19, 27, 76, 87, 88–89, 101
Lee, Rose Ann, 201
Leodas, Avra, 192
Lindgren, Eric, 243
Little, James, 207, 209
Living rooms, 74–97
Lomahatewa, Nieto, 213

Lonewolf, Joseph, 186
Long Hair kachina, 214–15
Los Cincos Pintores, 236, 239
Los Miradores, 50–51
Lostetter, Al, 245
Lugares de retiro, 122–29
Luhan, Mabel Dodge, 236
    house, 41, 146
Lumpkins, Bill, 42
Lutonsky, Paul, 248

M
Maitland, Richard, 240
Malo kachina, 213
Marquez, Bartolomé, 165
Martínez, Julian, 180, 185, 189
Martínez, María, 180, 182, 184, 185, 188,
    189, 191, 192
Martínez, Severino, 31
McCook, Sarah, 140–41, 218
McHugh, Kidder, 42, 44
McHugh, Lloyd and Associates, 97
McKenzie, Ken, 153
Medicine Flower, Grace, 186, 187
Meem, John Gaw, 41, 42, 44, 47
Mesa Verde National Park, Colorado, 12–13
Mexican colonial period, 30–31
Mexican tiles, 111, 114, 116, 118
Mexican War, 32
Middlemiss, Jon, 193
Mimbres tribe, 10
    pottery, 188
Mission churches, 24–27
Mojica, Luis, 209
Molleno, 29, 234
Monongya, Jesse, 207
Moorish design, 16, 28, 60–61, 64–65. *See
    also* North African architecture
Morang, Alfred, 236, 239
Morley, Sylvanus, 40–41
Moroles, Jesús Bautista, 231
Moya, Maria C., 208
Mruk, Walter, 236
Musial, Kalley Keams, 199

N
Nacimiento, 233
Namingha, Dan, 247
Nampeyo, 180, 183, 184
Nash, Willard, 236
Navajos, 22–23, 24
    baskets, 22, 174, 178
    jewelry, 22, 29, 204, 205, 206, 207, 208,
        209
    weaving, 22, 29, 194, 197, 198, 199, 200,
        201
Nichos, 62, 74, 167, 180–81
Nicola, Tim, 226
Nieto, John, 247
Nighthorse, Ben, 205
Nockadineh, Stella, 201
Nordfeldt, B.J.O., 236, 239
North African architecture, 44, 64, 71, 123.
        See also Moorish design
Nusbaum, Jesse, 40

O
Ogre kachina, 210–11
O'Keeffe, Georgia, 41, 236, 238
Ollas. See Baskets; Pottery
Oñate, Juan de, 24
Oraibi, 179, 212
Ornelas, Barbara Teller, 201
Ortega, José Benito, 232
Ortega Weaving Shop, 194

P
Pahlik Mana, 212
Paintings, 236–47
Palace of the Governors, 27, 38, 43
Panama California Exposition (1914), 38
Papago baskets, 174
Parsons, David, 221
Parsons, Leah Elizabeth, 192
Patrician Design, 138–39
Pawn jewelry, 205

Peacock, Carolyn, 248, 249
Pecos Pueblo, 29
    mission church ruin, 26
Peters, Bob, 113, 139, 145, 171
Petroglyphs, 14–15
Peynetsa, Anderson, 191
Phillips, Bert, 236
Phillips, Loren, 215
Pictorial baskets, 176
Pictorial rugs, 202, 203
Pima baskets, 177, 178
Pit houses, 10–11
Plains Indians, 32, 36, 222
Polacca, Thomas, 187
Popé, 26
Porches. *See Portales*
Portales, 27, 34, 148–61
Pottery, 10, 180–93
Pottery House, 43, 73, 102, 114, 125
Powamu Chief, 213
Pratt, Charles, 214, 227
Predock, Antoine, 42, 44
Prints. *See* paintings
Pueblo Bonito, 14–15
Pueblo Indians, 10, 16–19, 62
    conversion to Christianity, 24–26
    crafts, 28, 29
    pottery, 20, 180–93
Pueblo revival style, 41, 42, 46–47, 74, 157
Pueblos, New Mexican. *See* Acoma; Cochiti;
    Laguna; Pecos; Pueblo Bonito; San
    Ildefonso; San Juan; Santa Ana; Santa
    Clara; Santo Domingo; Taos; Zia

Q
Qöyawayma, Al, 186

R
Railroad era, 35–36, 52–53, 64, 68
Rancho de las Golondrinas, 7, 27
Rapp, Isaac Hamilton, 38, 41
Rapp, William Morris, 38
Rascon, Hector, 248–49
Retablos, 29, 233, 234, 235
Richardson, Nausika, 221
Riggs, Hillary, 218, 219, 221
Rio Grande, 8
    highlands, 16–19
    Valley, 191, 193
Rio Grande textiles, 29, 194, 199, 202
Rio Pecos, 37
Ristras, 71, 73, 108, 111
Robles, Ron, 240
Rodriguez, Billy, 248, 251
Rodriguez, Chalo, 248, 249, 250
Romero, Pedro, 229

S
Sakiestewa, Ramona, 195
Salas, 74–97
Saltillo, 194
Sandoval, Chris, 223
San Ildefonso Pueblo, 180, 184, 185, 188,
    189, 191, 192
San Juan Pueblo, 20, 180
San Miguel Mission Church, 26, 36
Santa Ana Pueblo, 183
Santa Clara Pueblo, 180, 185, 187
Santa Fe Archaeological Society, 38
Santa Fe Indian Market, 42
Santa Fe Museum of Fine Arts, 38, 231, 239
Santa Fe Opera, 42–44, 49
Santa Fe Trail, 32, 34, 62, 67, 98, 130
Santo Domingo Pueblo, 220
Santoniño Santero, 234
Santos, 29, 232–35
Sarkisian, Carol, 228
Scholder, Fritz, 76, 92–93, 240
School of American Archaeology, 38
Sculpture, 226–35
Seven Cities of Gold, 24
Sharp, Joseph Henry, 241
Shidoni Foundry and Gallery, 230, 231
Shook, Clorinda, 132–33
Shoshonean tribes, 16
Shuster, Will, 236

Sikyatki pottery, 183, 184, 193
Sloan, John, 236, 240
Smith, Richard Zane, 193
Soelen, Theodore van, 236, 241
Sombraje Collection, 141, 218–20
Southard, Charles, 230
Spanish Colonial Arts Society, 42
Spanish colonial period, 16, 22, 24–29, 47,
    64, 74, 98, 130, 194, 223, 232
Sprague, Roger, 240
Spruce Tree House, 13
Storyteller figures, 190
Strand, Paul, 41
Strell, Robert, 78–79, 130–31
Studio Arquitectura, 116, 117, 125, 171
Suina, Aurelia, 190
Sun kachina, 211, 215

T
Taos Furniture, 220, 221
Taos Pueblo, 18–19, 29, 50
Tapia, Luis, 232, 235
Tavlos, 246
Teec Nos Pos, 197
Teetzel, Bill, 219, 220
Territorial architecture, 31–37, 64
Terry, Karen, 129
Tewa, Dennis, 214, 215
Tewa pottery, 183, 187
Tewaquaptewa, 212
Textiles, 194–203
Thomas, Mary, 176
Tierra Wools, 194
Tohono O'odham baskets, 176, 178
Torivio, Dorothy, 189
Trasteros, 28–29, 101, 108, 130, 222–23,
    224, 225
Túhavi kachina, 215
Two Gray Hills Trading Post, 194, 200, 201

U
United States
    army architecture, 32, 98
    territory, 32–37
University of New Mexico, 40–41, 46, 247

V
Valdez, Horatio, 232, 233
Vargas, Diego de, 26
Veeder, John, 142
Vergara-Wilson, Maria, 194
Vierra, Carlos, 40, 41
Vigas, 19, 27, 60–61, 67, 71, 72–73, 93, 121,
    139, 140, 148–49, 156–57, 159, 160–61

W
Wade, Bob, 245
Wagner, Jim, 224, 225
Walls
    adobe, 16, 27
    masonry, 13, 14
    plaster, 27
Walton, Amy, 82–83
Watrous, Samuel, 34–35
Weintraub, Richard, 208, 209
West, Doug, 242
Weston, Edward, 41
Westwork Architects, 47, 54–55, 58–59, 91,
    126
Wetherill, Benjamin K., 13
We-u-u kachina, 212
White, Randy Lee, 92–93
Wide Ruins rugs, 201
Wright, Frank Lloyd, 73, 102, 114, 125

Y
Yavapai baskets, 175
Young, Judith, 207, 208

Z
Zia Pueblo, 182, 183
Zimmerman Library, 41
Zuni
    jewelry, 205, 206
    pottery, 180, 182, 191, 192
    villages, 16